What others are saying about...

UNLOCKING GENERATIONAL CODES

"Anna Liotta is *the* expert on what makes the different generations tick—and what ticks them off! In *Unlocking Generational Codes*, she shows you how you can get better results from the different generations in your business...and in your life!"

> – Bill Stainton, Author, *The 5 Best Decisions the Beatles Ever Made: A Handbook for "Top of the Charts" Success*

"Anyone who needs to communicate with anyone else—and particularly with people of another generation—absolutely *must* read this book! As a nearly life-long communication professional, I was surprised, and at times astounded, by Anna's insights on the differences in the generations. This book is an invaluable reference for everyone who wants to communicate effectively."

> – Evelyn Clark, Author, *Around the Corporate Campfire: How Great Leaders Use Stories to Inspire Success*

"This took me from clueless to having a clue."

> – Brian Walter, CEO, Extreme Meetings, Boomer

"The author's mastery of presenting complex material and generational issues in a clear, lighthearted manner translates into usable tips and strategies guaranteed to make a huge difference in any community."

— John Callahan, Pres. LBM Consulting, Traditionalist

"Finally...Being generationally different doesn't have to mean difficult."

— Erika Schmidt, President, Frause - Gen Xer

"As the leader of a company trying to reach a broad demographic market, I know how important it is to tailor the message to the audience. Now having read *Unlocking Generational CODES*, I know what I need to do to help my company communicate with and meet the needs of all the generations that are my customers and my employees."

— Paul A. Campbell, Co-CEO, bLife Inc., Gen Xer

"As a boomer boss managing a fast-growing company in the technology and social media industries, our entire company has benefited from the information in *Unlocking Generational CODES*. I've learned what inspires and drives my team and they've learned how upwardly to manage and motivate me. We all agree this is the key to our success."

— Steve Crandall, CEO, ProMotion Holdings, LLC, Boomer

"This book nails it. *Unlocking Generational CODES* offers insight about why it's harder to recruit younger people into organizations; it explains why people don't return phone calls, and why some folks would rather text than talk. It has unlocked for me some secrets of communication with everyone I meet. I wish I had this information years ago!"

— Tom Hurdelbrink, CEO , NWMLS

"In this age of technology, we often leave behind those unwilling to adapt. Anna Liotta has taught us why those of earlier generations are sometimes resistant to technology solutions, and how we meet their needs in a way that is customer-friendly and satisfying for all."

– Brett Alston, Managing Partner, Revel, Xer

"*Unlocking Generational CODES* made me rethink so many of my relationships, both personal and in the various places I have worked, be it academia, corporate America, or being self-employed, making me realize why I have had issues with younger and older employees, and how I can communicate better with everyone I meet. Most of all, it made me realize I'm not just some isolated hermit wannabe, but that my preferences for communication are very much the result of my being a part of Generation X."

– Tyler R. Tichelaar, Ph.D. and author of the
award-winning *Narrow Lives*

"In a long public speaking career, I've addressed rooms full of senior citizens and classes of college students. But only after I read *Unlocking Generational CODES* did I realize how much my message is primarily geared toward Gen Xers, and how I need to and can tailor my message also to Baby Boomers, Millenials, and all generations. This book is definitely the key to understanding the generations so anyone can achieve success in all aspects of business and life."

–Patrick Snow, best-selling author of
Creating Your Own Destiny and *The Affluent Entrepreneur*

DEDICATION

This book is dedicated with love to my father,
Alphonso Luigi Liotta.

My father is an extraordinary man who has taught
me so much about life, respect, human nature, and
the power of being positive. My greatest hope is that
my life reflects the brilliance of his
teachings and wisdom.

CONTENTS

HONOR THE LEGACY—
REALIZE THE POTENTIAL

Each generation has something new and vital to add to the elemental mix. Its contribution can only be realized fully when it becomes clear what motivates that generation's members, and what filters or personal paradigms they hold that could limit their possibilities.

Notice I say "could limit"—because no one is right and no one is wrong. True power becomes available when we have mastery in realizing how our paradigms and beliefs can actually create barriers and obstacles to our goals of creating a fulfilling, exciting future for our company, community, and family.

This book is designed for successful visionary people who are committed to improving themselves each day—successful people with inquiring minds and hearts who value human relationships and who want to understand better their employees, their customers, and even the special people in their lives, regardless of which generation they belong to.

This book is about how members of different generations think and act, but more importantly, its purpose is to increase understanding, insight, compassion, and success. The first three have everything to do with the final one—success. In the future, successful leaders are going to be individuals at every level of an organization who first seek to understand the attitudes, values, and beliefs of those around them, by asking such questions as: "Why they do what they do?" and "Why do they see the world the way they see the world?" and then using that information to determine what is possible for the future.

Next comes compassion: True compassion is not for the faint of heart; in fact only the strongest leaders and most effective advisors and sales professionals have the moral courage and integrity to be compassionate day in and day out with all their clients, colleagues, peers, and people. It seems so much easier to be "right" all the time and to do what benefits you without being concerned about others' feelings, wants, or needs.

But if being right and looking to your or your company's needs first is the strategy or technique that has sustained you or the people you know so far, you are about to witness the failure of that strategy in today's new marketplace, leaving you bankrupt and wondering what happened and what to do next.

To be effective and thrive in today's multi-generational marketplace, leaders must not only energize and motivate an age-diverse clientele and workforce, but they also must help them to deal with rapidly changing resources and priorities. This quantum task requires leaders to understand how individuals, teams, and clients—all with different Generational CODES—will respond.

Generational CODES can be used by leaders, visionary managers, sales professionals, advisers, and non-profit executives who want to be effective at bringing out the highest potential in their teams, colleagues, volunteers, and clients in these turbulent times of great challenge and great opportunity. In addition, understanding these CODES will help communication outside the workplace, in the home, and in personal relationships throughout society. Baby Boomers can use this information to understand better the Gen Xers, and the Gen Xers can use it to understand the generation of Traditionalists, who in turn may use it to help them better understand Millenials. Unlocking these Generational CODES will help to bridge the generation gap and benefit everyone in multiple ways.

What makes me, Anna Liotta, the person to convey this information and aid in unlocking Generational CODES? My exploration of how generational paradigms influence leadership and family began in childhood. As number eighteen in a family of nineteen children, I started to experience generational impacts on life at a very early age. After all, if you include my grandparents, parents, siblings, nieces and nephews and their children and now even grandchildren, my family's span of years covers all six generations alive today.

I didn't, however, consider how significant it was that I was raised in such a multi-generational family until my sophomore year of college. In my Organizational Development class, I saw a video that would change my life. The video, based on the work of author Morris Massey, was called *What You Are Is Where You Were When*. The video's message was that the events that happened in the world when you were ten years old forever influenced your worldview. I was astonished. Besides thinking about what happened when I was ten, I applied the idea to other members of my family. For the first time, I thought about what the world was like when my father was ten years old: The United States was in the middle of the Great Depression. My father was orphaned as a baby, so he would not meet his siblings and extended family until he was ten years old. As I began to think about how those events may have shaped his worldview and his parenting choices, I reevaluated my reactions to what I had perceived as his strictness and over-protectiveness.

My relationship with my dad was forever changed by that simple insight. An idea began to form within me that would take years to express, "What if we could all understand the formative events and core influences of the people we love, live and work with?" This book is the expression of those early nuggets of insight and joy that changed my life.

That video and the realizations that followed it led me to become more involved in generational studies, keynote addresses, training, and consulting. It became readily apparent to me that something was needed to provide a framework in which the power of understanding generational paradigms could be harnessed and put to effective use. After a number of attempts to create this framework to improve understanding of these paradigms, I discovered some general elements or categories for how members of each generation thought and acted, and if compared, these elements clearly showed how each generation approached family relationships as well as professional and other life issues. This approach resulted in identifying a number of elements, a prism if you will, through which generational characteristics could be identified and generally understood. The result of that framework and understanding is this book and the information it contains. I hope readers will find it a useful and insightful tool for bringing the power and knowledge of different generations to bear on personal and professional issues, and ultimately, for enriching our love and understanding of the people in our lives.

Anna Liotta

Seattle, Washington
September 9, 2011

PART 1

UNDERSTANDING THE GENERATIONAL MIX

1

THE PERFECT STORM

For the first time in history, we have six generations alive at the same time, each with its own viewpoints, values, attitudes, and beliefs.

GENERATIONS	BIRTH YEARS
G.I.s	1900—1926
Traditionalists	1927—1945
Baby Boomers	1946—1963
Generation Xers	1964—1979
Millennials (Generation Y)	1980—1999
Nexters	2000—present

(*Cusp Babies are four years on either side)

To heighten the pressure, the middle four of these six generations are actively working, competing, purchasing, and often colliding in the marketplace. This situation appears to be here to stay, and it won't be long before the Nexters will be joining the workforce. That the various generations will be working together for a long time was confirmed for me when I chatted with an expert at the Bureau of Labor and Statistics (BLS) in the Office of Occupational Statistics and Employment, who shared the Labor Force report projections for 2006-2016. The BLS researches the demographics and trends in ten year segments. If we start with what things looked like in 2006 and then project what the 2016 mix will look like, we are given a good preview of the generational mix on the horizon.

In 2006, our Traditionalists made up 15.6 percent of the active workforce. While many expected our Traditionalists to be exiting the workforce entirely over the next ten years, we can't count them out. The BLS projections have Traditionalists continuing to be a strong presence in the workforce in 2016, contributing 7.6 percent to the overall labor force. They are still working steadily (although often part-time to supplement their incomes), and they are unlikely to call in sick to go to a concert or sporting event with friends. And even if they are not part of your own workforce, you will surely encounter them among your suppliers and customers.

The Baby Boomer wave entered the workforce with a big splash in the 1970s. With high fertility rates and record levels of women participating in the labor force, we saw rapid growth of the labor pool until 1999. In 2006, the Boomers encompassed 32.4 percent of the labor force. And they are not moving into retirement as quickly as their predecessors. By 2016, Baby Boomers are projected to fill 27.2 percent of the workforce, more than doubling Traditionalists' participation rates at that stage of their working lives.

The BLS reports a number of trends that will keep Baby Boomers active in the workforce:

- Increase in the number of individuals living longer, healthier lives;

- Higher levels of education resulting in people participating in the workforce longer; and

- A move away from defined benefit pension plans toward defined contribution plans which give workers more incentive to remain working and contributing longer.

And as if these three were not enough, many Baby Boomers will be putting off their retirement for all of these reasons, combined with the devastating impact of the current economic crisis on the value of their retirement funds.

A BLESSING AND A CURSE— THE EXODUS OF BABY BOOMERS

For many companies, having the upper hand to select and reject talent through the tumultuous economic times of 2007-2011 has been a blessing. If companies' key managers and leaders have taken the opportunity to put into place the structures to transfer and capture the knowledge of senior executives and leaders to the organization's knowledge repository, they are in good shape.

If, however, the Boomers you employ—with their diminished 401Ks and increasing college costs for their Millennial children and underwater mortgages—have held their essential knowledge close to their chests to stay relevant, your company may face a huge problem.

A balancing act is definitely at hand. Boomers are uncertain how long they will want or need to stay in their positions.

Generation X began entering the Baby Boomer-dominated workforce as youths in the 1980s with limited success. By 2006, Gen X squarely shared the prime age worker stage with mid-to-late Baby Boomers, making up 22.8 percent of the workforce. In 2016, Gen X will briefly become the majority shareholder at 33.2 percent of the workforce. Gen Xers will be 37-52 years old, and serving as both leaders and prime age workers, bridging the abyss between senior Baby Boomers and energetic, innovative Millennial rising stars.

Our Millennials (Gen Y) have entered the workforce at a slower pace than any other generation. A number of factors influencing their entrance include: personal choices, rising family incomes, competition for available jobs, and increased numbers of young people attending and staying in school longer.

By 2016, they will be 17-36 years of age and will make up 32 percent of the workforce.

THE WIND, WAVES, AND CURRENTS

The diverse mix of generations in the workforce will pose continued challenges as we move out of the crisis of the Great Recession and begin to build again. Every generation feels a shock when it realizes it is no longer the rising energy of youth influencing the future, but in fact is now—gulp—"The Establishment." New generational currents are constantly at play in the marketplace so leaders need to be ready.

Starting in 2003, Baby Boomers began to exit the workforce faster than entry-level workers entered it. With 80 million Baby Boomers originally in the talent pool, many organizations became accustomed to having a strong bench of work-centric, competitive, self-motivated team players, but that tide is shifting.

As Gen Xers enter the stage of midlife, 42-64 years old, they are taking on the prime leadership positions in organizations and institutions. Mid-life is historically the time of an individual's highest productivity, earnings, and contribution to an organization. Many companies are at risk of losing their best Xers and don't even know it.

Over the next ten years, the demand for leaders between the ages of 35-45 will increase by 25 percent while the supply of eligible and interested candidates will decrease by 15 percent. According to research from the AARP in 2011[1], nearly one-third of the total U.S. workforce (32 percent) will be fifty years old or older within the next decade.

Decision makers daily confront the reality of a new mix of top talent in power positions. This "new breed" of young leaders can pick and choose where they prefer to live and work, choose with whom they like to work, and determine for themselves where they feel most appreciated. Companies are learning that not only do they not have a deep enough pool of Xers to fill their management needs, but often, their Xers are not interested in the management positions being vacated, and, in fact, plan to exercise their "free agent" status and move on to explore new opportunities and experiences.

USING GENERATIONAL SAVVY™ TO IMPACT THE BOTTOM LINE

Generational misunderstandings and friction can send human capital costs spiraling dramatically upward. So before you jump into the multigenerational traffic flow and get hit or cause an accident, you need to look both ways.

To make exciting futures possible, the focus should not be on our differences, clash points, or collisions, but rather on understanding the different generations' connecting points and common ground. The challenge is to shift our differences from causing problems into creating opportunities.

Powerfully working with each generation in a way that empowers and inspires its members is critical to your success. If you already know and implement such practices, you still may want to introduce such ideas to a colleague or manager who has a tendency to say such things as:

- If it ain't broke, don't fix it.

- They just need to learn the way we do things here.

- We will allow Facebook in the workplace over my dead body.

- They should be happy to have a job and stop whining.

Generational missteps often result in a loss of community and belief in the organization's vision, mission, and leadership. By recognizing what causes friction points and misunderstandings, we can significantly reduce costs including:

- Reduced profitability

- Loss of valuable employees

- High turnover costs and losses

- Wasted human potential

- Poor customer service

- Derailed careers

- Health issues caused by stress

In order to remain relevant and maintain a leading edge in today's marketplace, we must start by seeking to improve our intergenerational effectiveness. When properly applied, the elements of Generational CODES allow us to integrate each generation's formative experiences, events, and leaders with the social moods and natural life phases, which in turn, shape each generation and influence every aspect of that generation's professional and personal life choices.

When properly [thoughtfully, carefully, intelligently] applied…Generational CODES can help us to:

- Understand better the actions and motivations of others.

- Understand what others are trying to tell us.

- Help us be effective in getting our ideas across to them.

- Help others achieve their own goals and fullest potential.

- Mold a true team out of diverse individuals from different generations.

- Improve the bottom line.

It's all about how the members of different generations see the world through their generational lenses, their Generational CODES. True power becomes available when we have mastery in realizing how the paradigms and beliefs in our own CODES can actually create barriers and obstacles in supporting and advancing a fulfilling exciting future for our company, community, technology, and family. For example, you may be a Baby Boomer whose views are keeping the Millenials in your company from performing at their highest level because they do not feel appreciated. You may actually appreciate them a great deal, but how you express that appreciation may not be a way they understand or appreciate. Such miscommunication can affect productivity, employee turnover, and job satisfaction. By understanding Generational CODES, we can improve in all those areas.

REMEMBER THE MANTRA—IT'S NOT PERSONAL

Knowing what shapes the multigenerational mix as well as the state it puts us in can catapult you forward or be your downfall if ignored or mishandled. Often, it can feel like someone from another generation is personally reacting, ignoring, or trying to irritate YOU. Or, perhaps you may think the person personally doesn't like you or is refusing to agree with you. I can't say that never happens (some people may actually be trying to ignore or irritate you); however, many times their actions are rooted more deeply in their generational paradigm of how they see the world and believe that things should happen; this paradigm may include such things as what constitutes good work ethic, dress codes, and/or how people should be rewarded or disciplined in the workplace.

So as you continue forward on your journey of becoming Generationally Savvy™, I encourage you to use this mantra:

It's not personal—it's generational.

Read it again and say it out loud a few times. You may even want to visit www.UnlockingGenerationalCODES.com to print off a sign for your office or photocopy the last page of this book for a reminder.

It's not personal—it's generational.

In the following pages, I hope you will find much to interest you, but please don't be offended if you can't relate to every example, or you find one that makes you say, "Wow, that's a little too close to home." Often, a person in my trainings or in the audience will tell me, "Well, that doesn't sound like me." But later when we discuss it, we discover that what the person really meant was, "Well, I don't want it to sound like me, but actually it does. I just didn't want to admit it." Breathe deep and repeat mantra now...

It's not personal—it's generational.

THE GENERATIONAL CODES™

Understanding the Generational Codes and how they influence the life choices and intergenerational dynamics we face in the marketplace gives business leaders new insights and knowledge that lead to bottom line results.

While it is obvious to us today that cultures are different from one another because people grew up in different parts of the world with different influences, traditions, and belief systems, it has been less obvious that generational differences can be as impactful and deeply dividing as cultural differences without the proper understanding and respect.

Codes are cool, and often mysterious, therefore taking a bit of exploring and trial and error to get a handle on them. A lot like the generations.

So what are "Generational CODES"? When I use the term "Generational CODES," I am referring to an acronym for the five basic elements influencing and shaping the decisions, actions, and reactions of each generation. These CODES are the result of shared experiences during a generation's formative years.

The CODES form the basis and framework that the members of each generation use for making decisions about their personal and professional lives. The five key elements of the Generational CODES are:

C	→	Communication
O	→	Orientation
D	→	Discipline
E	→	Environment
S	→	Success

Element 1—Communication

The first element addresses the question of what is each generation's preferred communication style. How do members of that generation relay their messages out to the world? How do they prefer others to respond? What are the likes and dislikes of each generation when it comes to interactions, for example, in the sales process? What forms of media and mediums do they engage with most comfortably? For example, do they prefer to read the print newspaper or get their news on the Internet?

Element 2—Orientation

Orientation explains how members of each generation view themselves in relation to other generations, people, and the world. Do they feel connected and part of the bigger picture; secure and confident in the support they receive? Or do they

> WHEN YOU CRACK A GENERATIONAL CODE, IT GIVES YOU UNDERSTANDING AND ACCESS TO A WHOLE NEW WORLD THAT HAS ALWAYS BEEN THERE, BUT PREVIOUSLY WAS UNSEEN OR UNNOTICED BY YOU.

feel like they are constantly starting over from ground zero, trying to make a mark and carve out a space in which to belong?

Element 3—Discipline

This element focuses on the nature of productive relationships with authoritarian figures including: bosses, employers, parents. How do members of each generation interact with colleagues, family, and peers most comfortably?

Element 4—Environment

The fourth element looks at how generations deal with their environment. How do they engage with technology and space to work at their peak performance? For example, do individuals strive to have a private office with a door or want to hang out in groups on their laptops? It's important to understand not only human functioning and behavior but also the way we gather information, make decisions, energize ourselves, and relate to the world around us.

Element 5—Success

The last element addresses what success looks like for each generation. How do different generations measure success? What are the things they are willing to give up to attain it? What are the critical anchors in their lives, helping them to thrive and giving meaning to their lives? What are the deal breakers and the earth shakers? Does their success come from internal factors or external factors? Do they "live to work" or "work to live"?

GENERATIONAL CODES IS YOUR GUIDE

Using Generational CODES effectively allows leaders to release the essential elements of each generation that contribute and create extraordinary futures. The Generational CODES contained in this book are your guide to understanding the generations, leveraging their similarities and differences, and avoiding costly delays, disruptions, mistakes, and miscommunication.

Enjoy the journey to unlocking the Generational CODES and developing a distinct competitive advantage by leveraging your knowledge of: "What Makes the Generations Tick and What Ticks Them OFF."™

2

THE KEYS TO SUCCESS:
SURVIVAL TOOLS FOR YOUR
GENERATIONAL JOURNEY

The attitudes, beliefs, values, and expectations of each generation are the product of that generation's unique set of cultural, historical, and educational experiences. Those shared experiences and connections provide the basis for a fascinating and powerful set of Generational CODES that can help us understand ourselves, each other, and the world at large. Let me give you an example:

Last Christmas, I spent time at home with my dear parents who are in their nineties. One evening, we were invited to my sister's house for a potluck dinner. My mother lovingly prepared a casserole to share with the others and covered it with tinfoil. At the end of the evening, we returned to my parents' home, the now-empty dish covered once again with the tinfoil. Back in her kitchen, Mom carefully removed the foil, rinsed it, dried it, neatly folded it, and stored it to be reused at a later time. In her opinion, it still had several—perhaps even many—perfectly good uses left in it. Not reusing the tinfoil wasn't something she ever even considered.

As I watched her perform this simple act of thrift, I was filled with gratitude for all the sacrifices her generation has made on behalf of those of us who came afterward.

> GENERATIONAL MOMENT:
>
> A SPECIFIC ENCOUNTER OR INTERAC-
> TION WHEN FORMATIVE EVENTS AND
> EMOTIONAL RESPONSES UNIQUE TO A
> GENERATION SHAPE THE REACTIONS
> AND RESPONSES OF AN INDIVIDUAL.

What I was witnessing was a Generational Moment™. My sweet mother was a child of the Great Depression. The formative events and emotional responses she experienced from when she was eight to eighteen years old created deep imprints regarding what was right and wrong, good and bad, and "how things were done" that never changed for her, even though her own circumstances and the world in which she now lives have changed dramatically. Today, plenty of resources exist to buy another roll of tinfoil, but those experiences from her childhood, shared by many others born during that time, still shape her actions.

Let's look now at three examples of how generational differences in the workplace break down communication and cause problems and frustration for everyone involved.

Millennial Megan

Megan is a twenty-five year old rising star manager for an international women's fashion shoe store. Her staff turnover is 70 percent lower than the company average. She has quickly become a turnaround specialist and is often sent to under-producing retail stores to make them profitable. She has a 100 percent success track record.

Unfortunately, Megan's managers don't know she is planning on leaving. For the past six months, Megan's Gen Xer manager has been sending her terse e-mails focusing only on what else the company expects her to accomplish. The only positive feedback Megan has received has been in the form of pay increases and increasingly challenging assignments. Megan doesn't feel connected to her manager or to the organization. She doesn't believe her manager actually likes or even appreciates her. She sees the pay raises and difficult assignments only as a sign she is "making money" for the company. Megan wishes her manager would make time to come by the store personally or at least to call her on the phone and express appreciation for what she has accomplished. Megan knows she is a valuable employee, so she figures she can get another job with a company that truly appreciates its successful managers and makes them feel like they are part of a healthy family, not just a hatchet woman dispatched to clean up messes.

On the other hand, the Gen Xer manager believes the company is showing Megan how much it respects her by giving her freedom and space to do what she thinks is necessary. The company and her manager are not micromanaging her but just saying, "Here's what I want, and here's when I need it by." They are showing their appreciation through appropriate pay increases. That's what respect and appreciation look like from the generational vantage point of the Gen Xer manager.

NO RIGHT AND NO WRONG

GENERATIONAL SAVVY KEY:

NO ONE SET OF GENERATIONAL CODES ARE RIGHT AND NO ONE SET ARE WRONG.

When studying Generational CODES, it's important to realize this kind of scenario is playing out in workplaces across the world today with increasing frequency and frustration. Both Megan and her Gen Xer manager are doing what they think is right, but the result of not understanding each other's Generational CODES is leading them toward an avoidable loss of talent. Although both parties have the company's best interests in mind, the difference in how they approach the problem is about to become a costly one.

Baby Boomer Jane

Baby Boomer Jane, an executive vice-president in a large wealth management professional services company, wants to set up a meeting with high net worth Gen Xer Max. Baby Boomer Jane repeatedly telephones Gen Xer Max and finally catches him when his administrator patches her through to his cell. When Jane asks whether it's a good time, Max replies, "I've got five minutes right now."

Jane thinks to herself, "That's not nearly enough time to do justice to my work," so she responds, "How about scheduling lunch sometime soon?"

Max inwardly groans, thinking to himself, "No, not another networking lunch." He tightly replies, "If you can come to my office, I can carve out twenty minutes in two weeks."

Jane thinks, "We'll only have time to get to know one another. I wish we could meet socially to get to know each other, but at least it's a start." Jane responds, "Great, that works for me."

Two weeks later, Jane shows up in Max's office ready to get to know Max and share her philosophy, approach, and vision for serving her clients. Max has just returned from back-to-back road trips, working on a client proposal till 2:00 a.m., and dropping off the kids at daycare at 7:00 a.m. He's ready to get to the bottom line of what Jane has to offer.

Jane sees a picture of Max's kids on his desk and opens up the conversation by asking Max how old his kids are. Max says succinctly, "Five and two."

Jane continues on to ask more about his family and other "relationship developing questions." Max is desperately watching the twenty minutes slide by and thinking, "Would she just get to the bottom line? What does she have to offer me? I don't want to swap personal stories and anecdotes. I want to know what she can offer me. She's an expert; now I'd like to see some expertise."

After twenty-five minutes have passed, Max interrupts Jane's current anecdote illustrating her passion for client service to say, "I'm sorry; I have another appointment waiting." Jane attempts to make a follow-up meeting perhaps over coffee, but Max can't get her out the door fast enough.

As Jane walks away she thinks, "I can't believe how abruptly he ended the meeting. I thought we were really getting to know each other." Max, on the other hand, is thinking, "Why couldn't she just get to the bottom-line of what she could offer me? I know she's an expert; I did my due diligence before the meeting. Why did she waste twenty-five minutes of my time with small talk and her 'approach to client service'? If I didn't think she'd deliver good client service, why would I have talked to her in the first place?"

Baby Boomer Jane thought she was being effective in her sales techniques by taking time to develop a personal connection with Gen Xer Max. Unfortunately, Jane was going about it like a Boomer and Max's Generational Style™ of creating relationships in the sales cycle is vastly different! He wanted to start with a bottom-line first conversation about value and ROI. To Gen Xer Max, that is what creates the feeling of trust and relationship.

Gen Xer Joe

A regional engineering firm client came to me upset, confused, and worried. The Traditionalist and Baby Boomer partners had been privately discussing their leadership succession plan, which included Gen Xer Joe.

Joe, a talented and hard worker, is the son of one of the current partners. The HR Director was in a stunned state after hearing that Joe was leaving the firm after fifteen years of employment to move to another state and be a partner at a competitor's firm. The Boomer HR Director felt this decision had happened with NO WARNING and was now scrambling to figure out who would be the next person in line for succession.

When asked, Gen Xer Joe shared that during his tenure, no one had ever told him that he was viewed as the future of the organization, and his attempts to update and modernize the practices and programs were met with resistance. Meanwhile, the new firm had been quietly recruiting him by appealing to Joe's key Generational CODES. The new firm's partners were sharing their vision for the future openly and also encouraging Joe to cultivate and express his leadership ideas. The old firm's partners had excluded him from the dialogue since he was not a partner, and the firm's tradition was that input was only valid when it came from partners.

The new firm had already made adjustments to its company to create a flexible workplace culture that allowed Gen Xer Joe to have more freedom in his schedule, enabling him as a parent to spend time with his young family without the concern of being seen as having weak work ethic or being a poor team player.

What we have in all of these stories are unrecognized "Generational Moments" that left all parties frustrated. As you read this book and your awareness grows, you will likely begin to observe such Generational Moments. As your awareness and insight into the Generational CODES deepens, you will start to see situations differently. You may be in a meeting where you observe a tense, friction-filled interaction that you might previously have regarded as a personality clash when you suddenly recognize you are witnessing a Generational Moment. Both sides in the conflict

> EACH GENERATION HAS THE POTENTIAL TO BRING OUT THE BEST, AND UNFORTUNATELY, THE WORST IN THE GENERATIONS BEFORE AND AFTER IT.

are right. And unfortunately, from the vantage point of their colleagues' respective generations, both are wrong.

MULTI-GENERATIONAL GUIDE TO READING THIS BOOK

Each generation has the potential to bring out the best, and unfortunately, the worst in the generations before and after it. A key tool for supporting multi-generational people and goals is to help each generation to see itself in context with other generations.

As you read on, you may find that you are ready to move on to the next point or wish that this book went into more depth and microscopic stories with examples. Consider this in the context of your own particular Generational Style. How well does the shoe fit?

During speaking engagements, I have found Traditionalists and Baby Boomers generally love the personal stories I tell, and they often share their own with me during breaks. In contrast, Gen Xers will say they "liked" hearing about my family of nineteen children, but they really appreciated the bottom line practical and tactical information they could use immediately.

Each generation will find something different in this book that is more relevant and useful to its members and more reflective of their own experiences.

Traditionalists will look for the historical facts and stories that represent their experiences being honored and understood, or they will ask for my credentials and a letter of reference from others they already respect.

Boomers, our first generation of MBA holders, will look for the statistics, charts, graphs, or expert credentials to back up the information asserted here. Sharing my educational accomplishments, five plus word title, and significant awards would not go amiss.

Gen Xers will quickly get the gist and say, "Okay, now move on to the practical action, get to the bottom line, and show me some immediate value. 'Show me the money' with clear, concise examples I can use."

Millennials will want to know the latest and the greatest. If you can share it with me, I'm listening, but make it fun. The more stories that are about Millenials and their peers, peeps, and friends, the better! Whether they look good or bad in the story—are famous or infamous—either is better than being anonymous. Millennials may even initially want to skip past the information on other generations to get to the good stuff—"the stuff about them."

TERMS AND TOOLS FOR YOUR JOURNEY

**Natural Realities—something a generation takes as just an automatic fact of life. For example, Nexters do not know what it is like to live in a world without the Internet.

**Anchor Points—defining events that create an impression that shapes us. For example, for Traditionalists, the Great Depression is an Anchor Point.

Along the way, I will build on these terms and tools by providing illustrations that bring the generations to life through the different generational styles and learning formats, stories, and examples. I will share why each generation sees things the way it does, and what issues arise in attempting to make the generational styles compatible, or at the very least, understandable.

TICK/TICK OFF

Your competitive advantage in business lies in understanding, "What Makes the Generations Tick and What Ticks Them Off." A quick review of some key points is highlighted in the section Tick/Tick Off.

SNAPSHOTS

This section will provide an overview of the key developmental events, incidents, leaders, and points of impact on the formative years of each generation so we can better understand where each generation is coming from.

With these tools under our belts, it's time to advance in our journey so we can understand how different generations communicate in the workplace and in their personal lives.

3

THE PAST IS THE
KEY TO THE FUTURE

GENERATIONAL INGREDIENTS

Let's meet the generations that make up today's marketplace, each with its unique drivers and motivators. One cannot hope to become Generationally Savvy merely by dividing the existing population into convenient age groups. You need to examine not only the individual generation, but also, all of the forces that define that generation.

Each generation's formative years are filled with defining events, leaders, and social influences that affect the world around them. This combination of impressions made on a generation creates a generational understanding or perspective that remains with that generation's members throughout their lives. This cumulative perspective subsequently influences the attitudes, values, and beliefs of each generation regarding the outer world around them and the quality and priority of their inner world reflections.

> "HISTORY SHAPES GENERATIONS AND GENERATIONS SHAPE HISTORY."
>
> — WILLIAM STRAUSS AND NEIL HOWE, *THE FOURTH TURNING*

Looking at these influences from the perspective of a larger time scale, we can perceive that each generation is buffeted and polished by the winds of the prevailing social mood. The social mood that shapes a generation is influenced and defined by the historical events that were current during its formative years and the response of previous generations to prior events. It is essential that we do not try to isolate one generation as we seek to understand what shaped it, but to see it in relation to other generations it influenced or was influenced by.

Many events, moods, and seasons that occurred before a generation's timeframe, and which may be viewed as history to them, can still influence their daily choices and thoughts.

If we look back at a full lifecycle, approximately eighty-four years, we would find ourselves in a time immediately before the Great Depression. It was a time of gaiety as well as chaos spinning out of control followed by the Depression—a dark time. To us, the 1920s and 1930s may be history, but the economic events of the last few years (2007-2011 specifically) have caused the Great Depression to resonate with us as many people suffer through similar experiences that affect their pocketbooks and professional lives. If we are looking only at our present timeframe, many would say that recent events are just bad luck, random chance, a totally unconnected phenomenon. However, as noted scientist Carl Sagan says, "You have to know the past to understand the present."

The great news for leaders in the community, family, and business domains is that looking at the past with the right lighting along with a few educated filters can actually shed some insight on why we do what we do in the present, and perhaps more importantly, what we will do in the future. Forearmed with this knowledge, leaders can devise stratagems for the best way to lead, support, and advise us so we reach our goals with the most wins and the fewest bruises.

LIFE CYCLE STAGES

The timing of a generation is set by the average interval it takes a person to go through the first lifecycle stage from birth through childhood to young adulthood. In the United States, the age of twenty-one is recognized as the transitional point from childhood to young adulthood by a few rites of passage: graduation from undergraduate college, entry to a first autonomous job, and attaining the legal drinking age. The second stage is young adulthood, the third is midlife, and the fourth is elderhood.

FOUR STAGES OF LIFE

The four stages of childhood, young adulthood, midlife, and elderhood all have separate "job" descriptions, and the Generational CODES established during the formative years will be refined in order to deal with new accountabilities. Although the Generational CODES may become refined over time, they will always remain true to the basics laid down in the formative years, which according to historians Strauss and Howe, include:

Life Stage	Age	Social Role
Child	0–20	growth (receiving nurture, acquiring values)
Young Adult	21–41	vitality (serving institutions, testing values)
Mid-Life	42–62	power (managing institutions, applying values)
Elderhood	63–83	leadership (leading institutions, transferring values)
Bonus Elderhood	84+	dependence (receiving comfort from institutions, remembering values)

As generations move through different life stages and encounter the social moods of society's four-stage cycle, they will adapt their responses to the social mood of the time. These adaptations occur based on the Generational CODES that, as we have seen, are imprinted on each of us during our earliest stages of development. Knowledge of this process is the key that leaders need to manage effectively and to lead a multigenerational mix of people.

SOCIAL MOODS AND TURNINGS

Each generation also begins its journey of childhood to elderhood during a particular social mood. Historians spend their careers looking not only for facts and influences over time, but also natural patterns that recur periodically.

In their book *The Fourth Turning*, Strauss and Howe explain how "at the core of modern history lies a remarkable pattern: over the past five centuries dating back to the Reformation, Anglo-American society has entered a new era—a new turning—every two decades or so." At the start of each "Turning," people change how they feel about themselves, the culture, the nation, and the future.

A crucial opportunity for understanding human nature comes from understanding how each generation is shaped not only by the specific events of its formative years but also by adding the bigger role it has played in society's recurring social moods. Let's look first at how these four turnings are defined.

The Four Turnings, as described by Strauss and Howe, occur in the following order (I will provide examples for each one below):

High: When society is building and growing institutions and organizations. Prosperity is on the rise and possibilities are around every corner.

Awakening: This time is one of questioning and discovery. While High was focused on the external building of foundations with few questions asked, during Awakening, questions are asked and internal life comes to the forefront of importance. Young adults challenge the thinking and foundations of the institutions and organizations that were built during High.

Unraveling: Unraveling occurs when the cracks in the foundation created by the arguments and dissent of Awakening lead to fragmentation and uncertainty, hyper-individualism, institutional greed, and civic mistrust.

Crisis: This time is one of reevaluating values, priorities, and essentials. Society's focus is on survival and boiling issues down to the basic needs.

GENERATIONAL ARCHETYPES

As we have already noted, the social moods are cyclical. They also create a recurring reaction and response from the new generations that can be expected if not predicted when we look back at the last time this set of conditions was present in a former generation. These collective enduring responses of generations to the various social moods can be broadly called generational personas or archetypes. Each archetype or persona encompasses the current generation's core characteristics, reactions, and actions as well as the reactions and actions of prior generations in similar moods and cycles of history. Each generation's archetypes are shaped by when it enters into the rhythm of the social order. Archetypes lend balance and self-correction to the continuing story of America's generations as they are affected by what happened before their arrival and how they will influence what happens afterward.

Over the centuries, historians have consistently identified four archetypes that revolve in a cyclical rhythm. Historians Strauss and Howe coined the archetype names of Prophet, Nomad, Hero, and Artist. Their characteristics are as follows:

Prophet: Prophets are champions of great principles. They are best known for their coming of age passion and principled elder stewardship. Indulged as children, they become protective parents. Their principle endowments are the domains of vision, values, and religion.

Nomad: Nomads are pragmatists and bold results leaders. Nomads are known for adult years of hell-raising and midlife years of hands-on, get-it-done leadership. As under-protected children, they often become overprotective parents. Their principle endowments are in the domains of liberty, survival, and honor. As leaders, Nomads are cunning, hard-to-fool realists—taciturn warriors who prefer to meet problems and adversaries one-on-one.

Hero: Heroes are builders of great institutions. Heroes are known for their collective coming-of-age triumphs and achievements. Protected as children, they become indulgent parents. Their principal endowment activities are in the domains of community, affluence, and technology. As leaders, they are vigorous and rational institution builders. They are aggressive advocates of economic prosperity and public optimism in midlife and all have maintained a reputation for civic energy and competence to the very ends of their lives.

Artist: Artists are lifelong learners and flexible diplomats. Artists are best known for their quiet years of rising adulthood, and during their midlife years for their flexibility and consensus-building leadership. As overprotected children, they become under-protective parents. Their principle endowment activities are in the domains of pluralism, expertise, and due process. They have been sensitive and complex social technicians as well as advocates of fair play and politics of inclusion. They rank as the most expert and credentialed of American political leaders.

The four Archetypes each correlate with a particular season of life. Generations in turn correlate with Archetypes. For example, the G.I. generation began its childhood in the season of fall, a time of Unraveling. The Archetype for this season is the Hero. The same would hold true for the Millennial generation, also born in the Unraveling season.

The Baby Boomer generation, on the other hand, was born in the High season. For them, childhood is generally a time of bliss, abundance, and sunshine. They will generally exhibit the characteristics of the Prophet Archetype.

The following diagram illustrates the relationship between the Archetypes and the current generations. What is important for leaders to understand is not only the current season of winter we may find ourselves entering, but also, what this season will mean to each generation. What are the elemental strengths that each leader, team member, colleague, and family member will need in order to support and sustain him- or herself and the people he or she leads through this season and into the next?

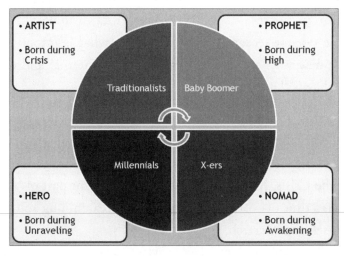

Generational CODES discuss the broad patterns of attitudes and behaviors common to people who are born and raised in the same or similar socioeconomic, cultural, and political time periods. In an unraveling social mood, pulling on the individual's thread is all it takes to begin to unravel the community's fabric. When a number of people begin to pull on one thread of personal greed or personal individualism, taking to excess, the fabric begins to unravel more quickly.

The social mood of each period moves from one tone to the next. The last social mood we were in moved from Unraveling to Crisis. Therein lay opportunities in the challenge. A Crisis is a time to go back to the basics. In a Crisis, we realize how far away we got from what was important. It is a time for appreciation and gratitude for the things we had begun to take for granted. During a Crisis, people come together in a new way and appreciate community, home, family, and the opportunities that their lives have provided for them.

THE LEADERSHIP IMPERATIVE OF THE CRISIS SOCIAL MOOD

During a Crisis period, business leaders need to reexamine the way they do business, the way they interact with their internal customers—their employees—as well as their external customers or clients. If people do not reexamine and reevaluate what is important and look for new ways to take care of both their internal and external clients, they will not survive a Crisis time.

At the end of a Crisis, the way of doing business—and the way we interact with the people we do business with—will be totally redesigned, so business leaders need to be willing to change and evolve during the Crisis. Although evolution is a constant part of business, a Crisis is a time of evolving and completely reexamining and recreating yourself from scratch.

The grief and stress during an Unraveling period leading to a Crisis period are a regular part of life. During this time, it becomes even more important to care for and nurture the community's fabric that was left to unravel because people feel socially disconnected during a Crisis time—they feel alone and insecure; they feel constant trauma and grief. They find it difficult to imagine others feel the same level of pain they do, and it's scary for them to imagine such because that would mean everyone is in trouble.

It's essential to keep communication channels open during a Crisis time so both authentic issues will surface and creative solutions from alternative channels may be shared, as well as offering a way to share to people who do not have a direct line for reporting problems to a senior leader. Frequently, people who have brought the problem to light may also have a solution when in other situations they would not be viewed as problem-solvers.

Leaders in a Crisis period often want to pull away, not speak out publicly or even speak with others. This withdrawing behavior is a mistake when leaders most need to be two-headed. On one hand, they need to keep clearing away the clutter of anguish, trauma, and upset so they can get to the root of the problem. On the other hand, they cannot cut out all community building, mutual mending, and group processing that happen when people assemble people together. If they try to cut everything away, the challenges will be turned inward and allowed to fester; individual frustrations will begin to grow and build. Small groups often can turn inward, and contamination from those small groups can begin to build. Then problems that could have been resolved by communication are allowed to grow and worsen.

THE UNRAVELING MOOD OF INDIVIDUALISM

The Unraveling social mood is a time of increasing individualism when, in general, people are watching out only for their personal interests, asking themselves: "What concerns me? How do I take care of me?" During this time, a few individuals can take down the whole structure because the power allowed them is turned into greed for the individual and neglect for the whole. The Unraveling time begins by pulling on the fabric of the overall society.

As that fabric begins to unravel, the whole Generational Constellation—the intricate mix of moods, events, and social changes that uniquely create each generation's CODES—is useful not only for understanding generational needs and responses, but also for preparing and planning for tomorrow's successes.

At such times, it becomes critical to understand the intersection between our life phases and the larger social seasons. The mood a generation is born into will be a major influence on the tone of events, the leadership focus, and ultimately, that generation's understanding and beliefs about how the world works.

Each generation meets the social moods in a different pattern and different phase of life. The social mood that prevails in each generation's childhood becomes the stage for the drama of its generation to play on for years to come. How we respond to the generations in their life stages and how each generation in turn engages society during its life stage helps write the script for the next play's scene.

GENERATIONAL CONSTELLATIONS

Boomers began their childhoods in the High social mood. It was a great time to be a kid. Adults, leaders, and civic organizations all invested in society's future with the children as the focus. No expense was spared and no effort was wasted to prepare, promote, and propel the children's advancement.

Xers started out their childhoods in the turbulent Awakening mood when the focus had shifted away from kids, thereby leaving children under-protected and left to take care of themselves. Society's priorities and obsession instead focused on the young adult Boomers and their hubristic youthful challenges to authorities and the institutional mores established in their childhood.

Millennials began their childhoods in chaotic and excessive Unraveling mood when society shifted back to a focus on protecting children. As the social fabric threads of the Awakening began to fray, leaders and institutions reorganized to celebrate the potential and support the well-being of kids.

Traditionalists and Nexters both entered their childhoods in a social mood of Crisis and scarcity. Society was focused on survival and dealing with the new basics. As the Unraveling gained momentum, the uncertainty of when the free-fall would stop caused fear, so the children were overprotected to the point of feeling smothered and tentative.

I mention both the Traditionalists and Nexters together because they provide an example of how history and these generational patterns repeat themselves. To gain insight into a generation's responses and patterns is to look back not five, ten, or twenty years, but eighty years, to the last time a generation with a similar theme to its formative experiences existed.

LIFE STAGE SHIFTS AND BIG SHIFTS

A life stage "shift" occurs when a generation moves from one life stage to another, and a social mood "shift" occurs when society moves from one season to the next.

During each life stage shift, the generations are moving from one life stage to the next. Each generation is moving away from playing one social role in the world and stepping up to the next role.

- Millennials are moving into Young Adulthood

- Xers are moving into Midlife (Power)

- Boomers are moving into Elderhood (Advising)

- Traditionalists are moving into Bonus Elderhood (Power—a new stage)

- And Nexters are entering Childhood

As each generation newly enters each life stage, it does so with its own unique agenda and perspective on what its mission or purpose involves. Although the younger generation is moving into a space that the previous generation occupied, that younger generation will not respond the same way the older generation responded because its unique set of Generational CODES will guide it. The new arrivals will make choices and follow or argue with older leaders based on their own formative experiences and interpretations of the world. It is essential for leaders and marketers to realize what a big mistake it is to think that this incoming generation will think and act a lot like the one that came before.

The "Big Shift,"™ one of the most critical times for the world at large, occurs when two fundamental changes happen in society at the same time, thus altering the world as we know it and the players in it. These fundamental changes occur as:

1. Each generation moves from one social role or life stage to the next, and

2. The social mood's tone and society's priorities shift.

Big Shifts happen every twenty to twenty-five years and fundamentally change not only the way we do business, but they also alter the way we manage and motivate each generation.

Currently, we are in the middle of these two major societal shifts. Business leaders have been feeling and dealing with these shifts even though they may not be entirely aware of the depth of their impacts or the potential for optimizing their possibilities.

OUR CURRENT SOCIAL MOOD SHIFT— UNRAVELING TO CRISIS

The current season (social mood) shift is from Unraveling to Crisis. Society is dealing with the impact of moving from a season of Unraveling—a time of individualism, institutional greed, and chaotic spending—into a season of Crisis where boiling everything down to the essentials is respected and demanded. Also, the power players in midlife are in the middle of a changing of the guard from the generational persona of Prophet to the pragmatic utilitarian "Just Do It" Nomadic style. The world will never be the same, and maybe that's good news....

It's easy for organizations to make the decision to cut resources in their communication and community building activities, but leaders beware. The great news about this Crisis social mood we have entered (according to the cycles, we'll be in it for the next ten or more years) is that we have the perfect alignment of generational elements to make magic. However, the true power lies in having a Generationally Savvy understanding that allows us to support the mix of generational elements in an optimal way.

During a Crisis era, the social mood and society's needs and focus are dramatically different from the Unraveling period. Leaders need to be supported through training to shift their ways of thinking and approaching problems. What is important for leaders to understand is not only the current season of Crisis, or winter, in which we find ourselves, but also what this season will mean to each individual generation that will experience it.

The Big Shifts we are engaged in today have us thinking and acting differently and turning the business world on its ear. This time of change makes it more important than ever to make friends and allies of people from all generations.

How does a leader lead, motivate, and assure individuals during this time? What are the elemental strengths that each generation expects and needs from its leaders, team members, colleagues, or family members to support and sustain it?

How leaders respond and work with people during a Crisis season has everything to do with the results they can produce. Leadership styles needed in a Crisis season are dramatically different from those required in an Unraveling season. In fact, leadership styles that worked three years ago could now be met with incredulity and disdain. This seemingly abrupt change in required leadership styles can be disconcerting to leaders who have perfected those approaches over the last fifteen years. Leaders must work to attract the best talent in these times and be effective in growing talent during this "Big Shift." Leaders must ensure that when the winds shift, the talent stays with them.

CURRENT GENERATIONAL CONSTELLATION

Each generation retains the persona of youth, but expresses it differently in different phases of life. A question that naturally surfaces is: "Where are we currently in this confluence of life stages and seasons?"

The G.I. generation is the outgoing Hero archetype. It is witnessing its second Unraveling and final Crisis stage. As bonus elders, its members feel very confident in sharing their opinions boldly and with authority. While their G.I. Bill, Social Security, and life benefits will probably last them through their remaining years, for the most part, they are now dependent on their children and grandchildren.

The Traditionalists have been the elders and advisors to the Baby Boomers during their loud and proud midlife reign as the holders of institutional power and influence. However, as we come to the end of the Unraveling and Big Shift from power to sage, Baby Boomers do not want to go quietly into retirement.

In the cycle of the generational seasons, Baby Boomers are a natural fit to win the "Most Likely to Succeed" nomination until their final phase. The Big Shift we are entering is the first time Boomers will really ask, "Wait, what happened to my charmed life?" As precious post-war children of a spring (High), they were pampered and applauded. As young adults of an Awakening, they were allowed to spread their wings and test their new world values and ideas with "free speech and self-expression." In their midlife, they dominated private and public institutions and the workplace in size, grandeur, and political clout. The final stage of shifting to the advisor and elder role does not sit easily on their shoulders or their self-perception. Giving up the reins and letting someone else drive and stand in the spotlight sounds like pure torture to Boomers. They will resist and work to reestablish new footholds in the marketplace, or if all else fails, reinvent what it means to be hip and senior.

The Boomers' saving grace, however, is that while they will have no qualms taking every last crumb of power they can away from the Xers (whom they've never really understood) their Millennial children will be an entirely different matter. They will move aside to make room for the Millennials, and while they are at it, they may just move right into their Millennial children's homes as well.

Gen Xers are moving reluctantly and skeptically into leadership roles. They are not seduced by power's promises. They actively want to avoid the ulcers and upsets that go with it, but they realize that their skill set of survivalist pragmatic leadership is just what these times call for to get us through the social mood of Crisis; therefore, they are stepping up to the call of duty, knowing that they'll never get credit, love, or props for what they do while they are doing it.

Millennials are chomping at the bit to go and do, to demonstrate their strengths and abilities and win favor and accolades for their valor and bravery upon whatever field of battle they are called to fight. As the new generation of Heroes, they need a cause for the greater good that is bigger than them, and the right leadership can bring forth and channel their intensity and energy into its full potential for good.

CURRENT SOCIAL MOOD—FULL CRISIS

Life Stage	Archetype	Generation
Elderhood	Prophet	Boomers
Midlife	Nomad	Xers
Young Adult	Hero	Millennials
Children	Artist	Nexters
Bonus Elderhood	Artist	Traditionalists
Bonus Bonus Elders	Hero	GI/ Veterans

To leverage the elements of each generation, we must be aware of how society's social mood and the life stages of each present day generation intermingle with each generation's formative core and generational persona. To understand fully a Generation's CODES, we need to travel back in time and learn about the events, icons, leaders, social mood, and life cycle season that shaped each generation. We'll turn now to some snapshots of each generation so we can get a better picture of its members—who they are, the way they were, and who they are today.

4

GENERATIONAL SNAPSHOTS

It's time now to look at examples or snapshots of each generation to reveal the elements that make up that generation's CODE, which in turn is the basis for how that generation perceives the world, its role, and that of other generations. When you get to the core of what people in a generation have in common—their shared experiences as a collective—you begin to see the big picture of why, as a generation, people do what they do, why they see the world as they see it, and how/why they lead, or micro-manage a project, relationship, or team.

THE G.I. GENERATION SNAPSHOT
NATURAL REALITIES IN A NUTSHELL

Born	1900-1926
Names	G.I. or Veteran
Archetype	Hero
Mood	Patriotism
Focus	Fighting the Good Fight
Technology	Radio, Telephone, Electricity
Shifts	Great Depression, Child Labor Laws, Women Voters
Beliefs	Buy American, obey your elders without question, save for a rainy day

NATURAL REALITIES IN A NUTSHELL

Anchor Points	World War I, Prohibition, Great Depression, Hooverville, World War II
People	JFK, Ronald Reagan, Walt Disney, Judy Garland, John Wayne, Walter Cronkite, Hitler, Churchill
Places	Normandy, Eastern Front, Western Front, Manchuria, Nazi Germany, Dust Bowl
Events	D-Day, Cold War, Manhattan Project, Resistance, 1929 Stock Market Crash

NATURAL REALITIES

The G.I. generation was born between 1901-1926. They make up less than 1 percent of the workforce. They were born during the Unraveling at the turn of the century and were known as "good-kids." They were our first Boy Scouts and Miss Americas. The chaotic times had adults instituting new rules to protect youth. Where the previous Lost Generation (Nomads) had struggled to survive amid child sweatshops and rampant social drug use, now authorities and parents were implementing child-labor laws and building playgrounds.

G.I.s had and still have a healthy respect for their elders and an appreciation for authority and rules. During the Depression, they patiently supported their parents, and as uniformed young soldiers, they fought valiantly in World War II to protect their country from foreign enemies "over there." As the heroic veterans of World War II, the G.I.s returned home to begin their careers with educations subsidized by the G.I. Bill. They were strong believers in the good and power of civil organizations and institutions. They earned their paychecks and built suburbs, miracle vaccines, plugged missile gaps, and launched moon rockets. As senior citizens, they have safeguarded their own "entitlements," but they have had little influence over societal culture and values.

TRADITIONALIST SNAPSHOT

NATURAL REALITIES IN A NUTSHELL

Born	1927-1945
Names	Traditionalists or Silents
Archetype	Artist
Mood	Compliance
Focus	Nuclear Families, Community and Civil Service
Technology	Radio, Silver Screen
Shifts	Rise of Labor Unions
Beliefs	Sacrifices for the greater good are necessary and honorable; hard work is its own reward; discipline saves lives
Anchor Points	Great Depression, World War II, Space Race
People	Joe DiMaggio, FDR, John Wayne, Ella Fitzgerald, Jackie Robinson, Colin Powell, Walter Mondale, Woody Allen, Sandra Day O'Conner, and Elvis Presley
Places	Pearl Harbor, Normandy, Breadlines, Victory Gardens
Events	Roaring Twenties, Two World War II, Hitler invades Russia, Great Depression, Hindenburg Tragedy, G.I. Bills, Korean War

NATURAL REALITIES

Traditionalists were born between the years of 1927-1945 and make up 7 percent of today's workforce. They are ready to retire and have been retiring. They are still an economic factor, and because of the changing economic times and improved quality of life, we are seeing some Traditionalists stay in the workforce longer while others reenter the workforce after a short stint in retirement due to both boredom and economic need.

Also known as "Silents," Traditionalists grew up during the double crisis of the Great Depression and World War II. Their Nomadic Lost Generation parents overprotected their Traditionalist (Artist) children almost to the point of suffocating them. While the preceding decades had seen times of abundance and gaiety, the crash of the stock market in 1929 launched the country into a Crisis season. Young Traditionalist children became familiar with the sight of ragged and hungry men fighting to survive wearing threadbare clothing and standing in soup lines.

By 1932, despite the promises made by President Herbert Hoover that "prosperity is just around the corner," unemployment was at 25 percent with nearly one in every four workers unemployed. The market had lost 80 percent of its value, and 9 million people had lost their life savings. With the addition of the most severe drought in U.S. history, hundreds of thousands of agrarian-based workers were displaced and drifting. Hoovervilles, the name given to cardboard box communities that sprouted up across the country, were a familiar sight.

These impressions and realities would never leave the young children's memories or allow them to take for granted the basics. You will never see Traditionalist grandparents buying daily $5 cups of coffee for themselves because of vivid memories of scarcity and conservation, but they will pay any amount for their grandchildren to have a better future.

BABY BOOMERS SNAPSHOT

NATURAL REALITIES IN A NUTSHELL

Born	1946-1963
Waves	1st Wave—the Draft, Vietnam War; 2nd Wave—The "me" generation—party (sometimes called "Generation Jones")
Names	Boomers, Baby Boomers
Archetype	Prophet
Mood	Prosperity

NATURAL REALITIES IN A NUTSHELL

Focus	Children in Spotlight, Growth of Business, Government, and Space
Technology	Radio, Silver Screen, Television
Shifts	Civil Rights Movement, Women's Liberation, Cold War, Rising Divorce Rates
Beliefs	There are not enough resources or chairs to go around. Competition is a way of life. Reach for the stars!
Anchor Points	Lunar Landing, Assassinations of JFK and MLK, Beatles, Vietnam War
People	Bill Clinton, Beatles, JFK, Deep Throat, MLK, John Glenn
Places	Vietnam, Chappaquiddick, Woodstock
Events	The Ed Sullivan Show, Watergate, Women's Rights, U.S. walks on Moon, Kennedy and MLK assassinations, U.S. sends troops to Vietnam, Cultural Revolution in China begins

NATURAL REALITIES

Baby Boomers were born between the years of 1946-1963. Also known as "Boomers," they were 80 million strong and were described as a "force of nature." Boomers have had an impact on every industry and institution they've touched.

The new post-war babies were celebrated and welcomed not only for the new hope and prosperity they represented but also as a reversal of the negative birthrate that had impeded the country's growth since the mid-1700s. G.I.s came home from the front in celebration, ready to start on the next big adventure, and together with their sweethearts, they would bring one bundle of joy into the world every seventeen minutes for nineteen years. With the advances in vaccines, infant mortality rates plunged and modern medicine was experiencing breakthroughs in pregnancy and delivery techniques with drugs that greatly increased the success rates of healthy deliveries.

The new financial prosperity and hard-fought-for peace and security were cherished, causing the new boom children to be nurtured and reared in a whole new way. Raised by guidelines outlined by the beloved pediatrician Dr. Spock, new Traditionalist parents and late G.I. moms indulged, doted, pampered, and encouraged optimism and self-confidence in this new Prophet archetype generation of possibility.

Organizations and institutions would forever be altered by the Boomers' needs, desires, moods, likes, and dislikes. Schools couldn't be built fast enough to accommodate the expanding numbers. Immediate post-war births were just the beginning; a second wave of youngsters was on the way. Three million more Boomers were born per year after 1950 than before it.

The post-war mood of growth and superpower expansion led to unquestioning trust in the government and big institutions. Baby Boomers were smack dab in the rising trend of middle-class families who were growing and prospering.

Little Boomers prayed in school and gathered regularly with family and neighbors to watch Walt Disney on the one color television in the neighborhood. They celebrated as Neil Armstrong took "one small step for man; one giant leap for mankind."

The High social mood was optimistic and positive as new miracle medicines were invented and the new frontier of space was just "one small step" away. This "can do" attitude spilled into the workplace, and the theme, "If you can imagine it, it can be accomplished" reigned.

Their work centric "Thank God it's Monday" philosophy and "Never trust anyone over thirty" attitude has 10 thousand Baby Boomers a day shocked to find out that they're turning sixty-two. In fact, for the next ten years, 10,000 Baby Boomers a day will realize they have a choice about retirement. To them, this is quite shocking! They don't even like the word retirement. To them, it sounds old, and they do not consider themselves old. Tammy Erickson, in her book *Plugged In: The Generation Y Guide to Thriving at Work*, tells us Baby Boomers are looking to retire the word "retirement." They prefer for words like "renew," "re-energize," and "refresh" to fill their language. Boomers confidently assert forever young language beliefs including "60 is the new 40" and in homage to the brilliance of Mark Twain: "Age is an issue of mind over matter. If you don't mind, it doesn't matter."

Boomers currently make up 42 percent of the workforce. Many of them want to leave the jobs they are currently in; however, many will not leave the workforce immediately. They will be looking for new jobs that are more rewarding and fulfilling both to their spirits and to their pocketbooks which will allow them to remain engaged and profitable. They like to call it their "entrepreneurial encore." When you help Boomers achieve their dreams of continuing to produce great results in their work while having a rewarding experience, you can expect great results.

GEN XERS SNAPSHOT

NATURAL REALITIES IN A NUTSHELL

Born	1964-1979
Names	Generation X, Xers, The Thirteenth Generation, Baby Buster Generation
Archetype	Nomad
Mood	Individualism
Focus	Leadership failures, Latchkey Kids, Consumer Boomers (Yuppies, DINKS)
Technology	PC/Computers, MTV, video games
Shifts	Politically Correct Language, AIDS Epidemic, Rising Divorce Rates, Title IX

NATURAL REALITIES IN A NUTSHELL

Beliefs	The world is not safe. If it's to be, it's up to me. Trust yourself; everyone else is suspect. Loyalty is an antiquated notion.
Anchor Points	Watergate, Stagflation, 1973 Oil Crisis, AIDS, Challenger Disaster, Fall of Berlin Wall, Wall Street frenzy, Dot-Com, Persian Gulf
People	Bill Gates, Quentin Tarantino, Madonna, Michael Jordan, O.J. Simpson, Johnny Depp, Barack Obama
Places	Iran Hostage Crisis, Cannes Chernobyl, Iraq, Wall Street, Check Point Charlie
Events	Crack, AIDS, Desert Storm, Watergate, Berlin Wall Falls

NATURAL REALITIES

Xers were born between the years 1964-1979. Only 44 million born Xers make up 29 percent of the workforce today and are in their peak earning and young family years.

Xers were the children of the first wave of Baby Boomers who work twenty hours a day and bled company colors. Both mom and dad were in the workforce, so these adult, former latchkey kids, don't want their children to have the same lonely childhoods. As a result, they're looking for a balance between their career goals and their family goals, and they are not willing to sacrifice their children's childhoods.

Gen Xers survived a hurried childhood of benign neglect and low expectations. Growing up in the long shadow of the Baby Boomers, Xers were largely ignored or criticized for not being more like the Boomers.

With an Awakening social mood in high swing, the priority had shifted away from fostering the child and was firmly mesmerized by the rants and chants of idealistic young adult boomers. Generation X was born into what author Tom Wolfe labeled the "Me Decade"[1] (the 1970s). The "Me" focus, however, was on the young adult Baby Boomers and left the Nomadic Xers to survive as they could.

From Woodstock to Watergate, Xers felt the brunt of Boomers exploration. The "Happy Days" of childhood to Xers was a sitcom on TV. With both men and women entering the workforce at nearly equal rates, this was the first generation whose parents openly tried to prevent pregnancies by taking a "pill" approved by the FDA in 1960.

To support the appetites of the "Decadent '80s" consumption-focused culture, many families opted for a two-income household, leading 50 percent of mothers into the workforce. Economic freedom for women was on the rise. Divorce rates tripled to over 50 percent, and soon nearly 40 percent of Xers were raised in single-parent households. Xers were four to five times more likely to have experienced divorce in their families than their Boomer predecessors.

With social programs and after-school activities lagging behind the need, Gen Xer latchkey kids went home after school to an empty house to fend for themselves.

The nightly news frequently featured raw and unfiltered stories about a television evangelist or politician playing by a new set of rules both morally as well as legally. But it really did not seem to matter to anybody as breaking the rules or living by your own moral compass was becoming the new norm.

Leaders and institutions were no longer to be blindly trusted; now it was each man, woman, and CHILD left to watch out for him- or herself.

At the same time, Gen Xers' Boomer parents were struggling with illusions and dissolutions as they began to relinquish many of the idealistic ideas and ideals of their "hippie" social change days for all the benefits of a "yuppie lifestyle." Long hours, tricky politics, and family time sacrifices were all navigated carefully with the implied promise of future promotions, corner offices, and premium parking.

It all came to an abrupt head with Black Monday on October 19, 1987 when stock markets around the world crashed. But the Boomers rebounded and continue to live the good life of fast money, fast deals, and precarious balance that each Prophet generation leads in its mid-life stage of the Unraveling period that leads us into the next Crisis Social Mood.

MILLENNIALS SNAPSHOT

NATURAL REALITIES IN A NUTSHELL

Born	1980-1999
Waves	1st Wave—Internet evolution, World Wide Web; 2nd Wave—9/11 and Social Media Home
Names	Gen Y, Millennials, Echo Boomers, Net Generation
Archetype	Hero
Mood	Excess
Focus	Trophy Children, Rhetoric of Empowerment, School Violence, Deregulation
Technology	Cell phones, Internet, Texting, Reality Television, Social Media, "Real-Time"
Shifts	Good Kids—Kinderpolitics, Soccer Moms (Dads, too), "It takes a Village," Girl Power
Beliefs	I am a precious gift from God. My parents wanted me. I've got options. I can be famous.
Anchor Points	Columbine, Virginia Tech, Oklahoma City bombing, 9/11, Katrina, Tsunamis—Sri Lanka, Japan
People	Prince William, Chelsea Clinton, Kurt Cobain, Leonardo DiCaprio, Venus Williams, Serena Williams, the Olsen Twins, Tiger Woods, Dakota Fanning
Places	World Wide Web, MySpace, Facebook, YouTube, Twitter, Africa, China
Events	9/11, Columbine, Virginia Tech, Oklahoma Bombing, Katrina, Tsunamis—Sri Lanka, Japan

NATURAL REALITIES

Millennials were born between 1980-1999. Although we will call them Millennials, other popular names that float around include Generation Y and Echo boomers. This high energy, extremely connected, and engaged generation of young people will tell you they are not an echo of anyone. They are not just the next letter in the alphabet.

Millennials are a whole new breed at 76 million strong and 22 percent of the workforce. Only 50 percent of the Millennials have entered the workforce so far. If you think their Boomer parents changed the way things were done, watch out; here come the Millennials! In the year 2010, we turned the corner to having more Millennials alive than Baby Boomers.

The Millennial Generation is a large generation, and consistent with the Baby Boomers' generation, it also has two waves. The first wave is called the digital divide, and their parents are predominantly Boomers. The second wave, the social media wave, has mostly Gen Xer parents.

That's one aspect of what creates the waves parents, but when we go to influences of technology, we see the first wave of Millennials, the digital divide, who are integrating the new media of the computer and the Internet. The second wave of Millennials always had the computer and the Internet as part of their lives, an integral part of their education, and they're the generation wave that will only know a world connected through social media. They are the generation that will say the people I know as my friends not only live in my neighborhood but live around the world.

The two elements that create the waves are parents and technology. The first wave of Millenials, the digital divide, are integrating the new media of the computer and the Internet.It will become essential to organizations to understand that knowledge management is both about technology, and the culture that it creates—the Millennial culture.

Millenials were raised as the first digital natives generation. Hyperconnected from childhood through young adulthood, Millennials grew up with technology in their schools, in their homes, and in their social places of play. They will find it difficult to understand why senior generations don't see technology as the answer to most problems. The fact that every other generation was introduced to technology after its initial formative experiences, and thus were digital migrants, does not truly compute for Millennials.

Technology that Millennials have at home they now expect to have not only in their schools, but in their places of work at the same level, and it can be incredibly frustrating when there is subpar technology in their jobs.

Millenials' social networks have become their way of creating neighborhoods, their way of creating connection. They give social networks and digital connection the same weight as face-to-face.

Millennials arrived as the newly cherished "gifts from God." The vast majority of the pregnancies of Millennials were planned by their parents and often at great cost. Millennials have always felt loved and wanted by their parents, teachers, and school leadership.

Wherever they've gone, they have been received with open arms. Millennials have a large spread in their parents' ages. They were born from single, unwed moms to early start Xers to Baby Boomers who postponed having children or are on second chance families (and sometimes third) leading the charge committed to getting it right this time.

Whoever the parent, in the Millennials' childhood, it was a good time to be a kid again. A resurgence of the positive focus on the child shifted adults' attention to everything "pint size" with the emergence of Baby Gap, Toys"R"Us, and Gymboree.

As adults became dissatisfied with the quality of public school attention on their "little miracles," a new trend toward private schools for the middle class and home schooling provided Millennials with every opportunity.

Across the globe, the reputation of children was positively reinvented. The Millennials helped rebrand children as media darlings and moguls. Not since post-World War II High times had it been so good to be a kid.

However, the prevailing Social Mood of Unraveling continued to impinge on the rose-colored hue that Boomer parents wanted to cast on their children's experiences and teachings. Children learned about "Stranger Danger," and unified programs like Amber Alerts were put in place. Kinderpolitics became popular with the themes of "It Takes a Village" and "No Child Left Behind" reigning.

The new focus on personal and public safety would escalate to an entirely new level for Millennials as they dealt with the events of the Columbine massacre in 1999, September 11th in 2001, and the Virginia Tech killings in 2007. These tragedies not only affected their country but people their own age. Not since the Civil War had a U.S. generation seen so many deaths of peers its own age happen on its own soil.

Millenials also grew up when family values was a popular term again. It was all about the politics of spending time with kids. There even became a word about kinderpolitics. Everything became referenced by asking, "How does this affect kids?" Contrary to the time of the Gen Xers, Millenials now were prize young darlings, so they became the focus of rules, of laws, of protection, and of celebration.

Disney became a leading edge of this shift. It started out with movies that celebrated happiness and joy and moved to movies that celebrated children being smart, and children being smarter than adults. Disney's *Spy Kids* focuses on kids who figure out how to save the world from the bumbling adults who also need saving. Clean-cut is back in vogue, along with purity rings that tell the world you are morally virtuous and you've promised your parents to stay that way.

NEXTERS SNAPSHOT

NATURAL REALITIES IN A NUTSHELL

Born	2000-Present
Names	Nexters
Archetype	Artists
Mood	Sensitive
Focus	They worry about saving money with their parents, wearing their bike helmets, using sanitizing gel, getting the flu.
Technology	iPods, iPads, Cloud computing, Global Access
Shifts	Diversity, Strangers are Dangerous, Your every action hurts or helps the environment
Beliefs	Children around the world are my friends, peers; we are global citizens
Anchor Points	Pandemics, Amber alerts, Great Recession, Hand Sanitizers, Bike Helmets, Schools Closures due to Flu

NATURAL REALITIES

Nexters were born in 2000 and after and can be described as sensitive artists, overprotected, and ethnically diverse. They have been taught such lessons as "Never leave home without your helmet." Nexters are children of the Crisis with "Stranger Danger," Amber alerts, and pandemics being regular occurrences in their daily lives.

Due to the state of the economy, they think about saving money with and for their parents. They are hearing about radiation spills and the celebration over the death of Public Enemy #1 Osama Bin Laden.

They also are seeing a President of the United States of America who could be any one of them—humble beginnings, broken family, poverty and mixed race, but still able to create a path to success through hard work and persevering to the end.

SOCIAL MOOD CYCLES

| Generation | Constellation Trajectory | | | |
	Childhood	Young Adult	Midlife	Elderhood
GI Gen.	Unraveling	Crisis	High	Awakening
Traditionalist	Crisis	High	Awakening	Unraveling
Boomers	High	Awakening	Unraveling	Crisis
Gen Xers	Awakening	Unraveling	Crisis	High
Millenials	Unraveling	Crisis	High	Awakening
Nexters	I have left off some of the other categories for Nexters because they are still too young for us to determine those details.			

WEAVING THE THREADS TOGETHER

Each thread of a generation's formative experiences influences its communication, leadership, and purchasing decisions today. Those formative experiences become a sounding board used by each generation to formulate its life priorities, community engagement, relationship styles, and nature along with many other decisions. The basis and framework a generation uses to choose, monitor, reward, and advance its work, family, and fortunes are revealed to us as we examine each of the elements of their Generational CODES. With this in mind, we are now going to examine the CODES: Communication, Orientation, Discipline, Environment, and Success Factors.

PART 2

GENERATIONAL CODES

5

COMMUNICATION

Three colleagues at a Research University were having a discussion about phones after one of my Generationally Savvy Trainings™. The first person, a Baby Boomer, expressed frustration that her Xer children expected her to be attached to her cell phone and respond to their photos of the new grandbaby immediately.

The Xer teaching peer joined in and said, "I can never get my parents (Traditionalists) to remember to turn on their cell phone. They only have it for emergencies, so they turn it off unless they are having an emergency. They think it's rude and intrusive to have someone call them when they are out with friends, but if I'm having an emergency, I can't reach them!"

The Millennial student piped in saying, "My parents (Boomers) get so frustrated with me because when I see they called me, if they didn't send me a text, I hit call back. It's so efficient, but they are ticked that I didn't listen to their message. Messages take so long; what's wrong with a quick text to tell me what they want?"

Sound familiar?

THE OSTRICH APPROACH IS NOT AN OPTION

While we might disagree about what communication tools are the best to use and when it is appropriate to use them, Traditionalists, Boomers, Xers, and Millennials can agree that changes in communication are reshaping every aspect of our lives. Each generation tends to see the effectiveness and appropriateness of various means of communication differently, often causing friction and fraction in the workplace.

COMMUNICATION OF THE INDIVIDUAL GENERATIONS

Technology has always been viewed as a mixed blessing. While it provides new efficiencies, and ultimately, an increase in productivity, all through history it has also brought great frustrations and challenges to the comfort levels and security of the more senior generations in the workforce.

From our twenty-first century perch, today's fast-paced, plugged-in world contrasts so starkly from the slower paced and seemingly more personal world of yesteryear. Technological advancements zipping toward us at Mach speed have created a cultural revolution in communication and a crisis in professional and often personal interactions among the generations.

Of all the generations, Millennials and Nexters have been swimming in bits and bytes their whole lives, and to them, it's as natural as breathing. While I was in Europe writing this book, my lovely friends whom I was staying with got two iPads fresh off the assembly line. Their Nexter daughter immediately began to play with one; she quickly figured out how to unlock it and get to her programs, becoming obsessed with it to the exclusion of adults. She never asked, "How do I do this?" She just kept trying new things until the results she wanted happened. Meanwhile, the adults kept asking the technology expert, "How do I….How do I…?" on every new nuance that we hadn't experienced before. Unwilling and worried about trying to figure it out by trial and error, we Baby Boomers and Gen Xers remember with horror the days of the little black bomb that came on the screen warning you of BIG TROUBLE.

Traditionalists: For Traditionalists, face-to-face contact was a norm for isolated lives in predominantly rural, agrarian communities. Families sat around the radio and listened to recognized authorities, like Walter Cronkite and Edward R. Murrow, deliver the news. For Traditionalists, most communication technology has been seen as a necessary evil that often gets in their way of doing things the way they've always been done.

Boomers: The golden age of television dawned providing passive and solitary entertainment for the individual or family. At work, information was scarce, expensive, institutionally oriented, and designed for passive use with "reasonable" turnaround times.

While most Boomers never saw a computer in high school or college outside of the science classrooms, the advent of big computers had Boomers parading around their college campuses to protest the lack of recognition of their individuality wearing cards saying, "Do Not Fold, Spindle, or Mutilate."

Gen Xers: Shaped by a time of mass marketing messages blaring on the television, radio, and now the Internet, Xers were surrounded by a culture of gadgets and tools that delivered instant results in short sound bites. With the introduction of cable programs like *Sesame Street*, young Xers were entertained and engaged as they learned their letters and lessons in short, diverse segments of programming specifically crafted for them.

As the new television network, MTV, hit the airwaves, Xers were now the first generation to be directly targeted in commercial marketing. With over 3,000 sales impressions hitting them daily, Xers quickly became experts at deconstructing and cutting to the core of the advertising hype.

Today, Gen Xers view all advertising with a critical and somewhat jaundiced eye. They appreciate when marketers and advertisers respect their savvy and approach them with quirky interesting messages that have value, transparency, brevity, and directness.

Xers were the first generation to use personal computers in college and on their first jobs. With new levels of public access to the on-ramp of the World Wide Web, Xers found themselves partnered with young second-wave Boomers for a short, high-energy thrill ride at the center of the spotlight of the dot-com. The race was on to find ways to monetize the abundant cheap access to information, make it personally oriented, and leverage its capacities to support making quick decisions.

By comparison, Boomers had ruled with the philosophy of "Information is Power" so hold the information close to your vest. In his book *Generation Blend: Managing Across the Technology Age Gap*, Rob Salkowitz, says, "Some Boomers also perceive new collaborative content and distributed decisions-making technologies as a threat to their hard-won authority." Xers adopted a new tact. With only 44 million peers ever born, Xers knew they couldn't compete in numbers. However, they could compete by turning the philosophy around and saying, "Creating and sharing easy access to information is powerful, and profitable too." We have seen Xer-led organizations such as Google, Amazon, Yahoo, Craig's List, Salary.com, and Pandora enter onto the world stage, capitalizing on the information power equation.

Millennials: Millennials have grown up as the first generation of digital natives. Communication for them has always been a natural and connective tool. While their Xer siblings may have been the first to have personal computers, Millennials have had access to the Internet, cell phones, and e-mail since they were in diapers. The world of information is at their fingertips and they pride themselves on being able to find information at Mach Speed.

They have naturally been making paths into global diplomacy from random e-mail pen pals around the world in first grade to visiting the corners of the world through the virtual highway of the World Wide Web. For Millennials, communication is all about 24/7 access, self-expression, and getting it done fast. They don't wait for anything (or anyone). They feel they just need to give you enough information for you to get to the meat of the matter, and that's it.

> TRADITIONALISTS: Relationships are power
>
> BOOMERS: Holding information is power
>
> XERS: Sharing information is power
>
> MILLENNIALS: Knowing where and how to access information fast is power

COMMUNICATION CHANNELS, WAVES, AND FILES: IT'S NOT ABOUT EITHER/OR BUT BOTH/AND

Communication is continuing to trend toward being an informal, fluid, asynchronous moving target. Traditionalist and Boomer managers may want to argue that texting and technology are cold and impersonal. For Millennials who grew up swimming in bits and bites, face-to-face is just one communication option, and they often don't believe it is the most effective or time-efficient option.

Informal and cost-effective digital access solutions are leveling the global playing field at an exponential rate and removing historic barriers to doing business. The use of technology as the ultimate answer to business questions can seem threatening to Boomer and Traditionalist generations who have gathered twenty-five years of "experience" becoming experts at doing it the "right way."

Traditionalists and Boomers might see these new means of communication as lacking the personal, humane, or intimate quality that healthy relationships require, arguing that you cannot get to know someone through a computer, website, or text; it's impersonal. On the other hand, many Xers and most Millennials will view these forms of communication as offering even more avenues to deepen meaningful connections to be built on in the future. How we integrate and leverage the power of both old and new technologies and face-to-face connection points can make all the difference between success and failure. Here's an example:

> An international telecommunications company released an ad in 2009 of an adorable, young Nexter girl walking through her neighborhood posting photocopy pictures of her lost dog. A mid-teen Millennial boy watches her post the picture on a telephone pole before she dejectedly walks away. The Millennial boy then pulls out his smart phone, snaps a shot of the dog's picture, and text messages it out to all of his friends. We see all of his friends receive it and forward it onto their friends. Within seconds, someone from the network of friends who is petting a lost dog gets the text and picture and responds that the dog is found. By the time the young Nexter arrives back at her home, the Millennial boy and dog are already waiting on her porch steps.

While the original point of awareness about the lost dog came from a standard lost dog poster, the Millennials leveraged their digital connectivity tools to speed up the successful outcome. Today, both Millennials (and Xers too) are ready and hungry to find ways and sponsorships for proactively integrating digital/social media interactions with face-to-face solutions. While it can make Boomers and Traditionalists a little nervous to feel like there are unknowns about which they are not experts, it's essential to consider the equality or even superiority of digital/social media solutions for getting the job done.

CROWD SOURCING: CHEATING OR LEVERAGING YOUR RESOURCES?

Millennials will argue that their open dialogue via instant messaging gives them access to a resource-rich group of friends that saves them time. Often, they will ask a quick question sent out to a large community and have a response back instantly that can save them hours of looking for information. A quick text or IM is much better than a random Internet search. But this method can also be a sore point when they use such an informal tone of asking for free information for review from a superior at their workplace, or their helicopter parents.

SOCIAL MEDIA AND REACHING YOUR CUSTOMERS

Most of us are used to selecting the radio or TV station we prefer to receive our news or entertainment through while dabbling in or surfing others. Generally, we return most frequently to the channel that presents the information the way we like best to hear it.

Today a myriad of available channels makes selecting the right mix for an advertiser an art. While you might find yourself trying to redirect people to the channels where you play your message, the key to getting your message heard is being willing to play/place it where the ears and eyes of your customers migrate, even if you don't like that channel, or understand why they go there.

For example, if your customers really like country music and listen to country music 24/7, but you play your message on a classical music channel, your customers will never hear your message. Even if it's a really good message and they would love what you have to say, you're not playing your message on the channel they regularly listen to. Empirically, one form of music is not superior or inferior; however, each of us has our preferences. When you seek to attract, grow, and retain clients and employees, you have to learn what channels they listen to and trust.

Social media is similar. People are finding their channel of comfort. For some it's Facebook, with the chatting and informal nature, like having a conversation in your living room. Facebook dialogues can, and often do, slip into business, but most frequently, you are chatting (as you might over beverages) with friends about their lives, experiences, and dreams.

For others, it's Twitter with the rapid short updates, bursts of information, and quick trends that reflect the hot topics of the moment. Topics swell and crest, then ebb away, but if you missed the wave, you can always search it out later with the right hashtag (#).

YouTube is for the visually compelled. The number two search engine after Google, YouTube has found a home in the hearts of Millennials and others alike. Need to see a baby laugh, a dog skateboarding, or a kitten playing with a dolphin to brighten your day? It's a mere click away. Want to find out some information on a random topic? YouTube's got you covered.

Generationally Savvy Solutions to Reaching Customers via Social Media: No one channel is the only dominant or final word for all of your clients' interests. Think of social media like the sandwich boards businesses put out on high traffic roads to direct people to their business. Every real-estate broker knows the value of a compelling sign strategically located. As a business leader, investigate your ideal customers' social media community preferences and patterns, and place your value-based message there.

An example of how one company used social media to reach its customers is Dell computer's use of Twitter. Dell realized Twitter's power as a cheap and powerful tool for providing value and making a profit. When Dell had a huge surplus of refurbished computer "stuff," it put it out on Twitter as a customer service FYI and the word spread virally. Profits soared and customer satisfaction went with it.

THREE SIMPLE RULES OF SOCIAL MEDIA

When using social media, be sure to promote your message "respectfully." It's important to investigate the community tone, rules, and protocols before you jump in since each form of social media has definite ways to participate and ways to get in trouble. Here are three simple guidelines when using social media to market to your customers:

- Don't endlessly and bluntly hawk your products and services.

- Be generous. Give free information, solutions, upfront value.

- Don't steal great ideas and pass them on as yours. It's great to ReTweet (RT), but always give attribution as the community of social media is self-policing and its members will call you out.

COMMUNICATION PREFERENCES BY THE "GENERATIONS"

Media	Traditionalists	Boomers	Xers	Millennials
Face-to Face	High	High	As Needed	Sure, Why Not?
Hand-written Notes	High	Strong	Neutral	Nice
Facebook	Low/But Growing	Grows with Grandbabies	Evolving	Top Priority –Home
Linkedin	None	Evolving	High Priority	Growing
IM/Instant Messages	Low	Low	Medium	High

Media	Traditionalists	Boomers	Xers	Millennials
Text Messages	Low/But Growing	High w/Teen Kids	Growing Rapidly	Essential
Voicemail	Diligent to Neutral	High	Prefer E-mail	Use as caller ID
Websites	Neutral	High	Basic Facts	Secondary to Social Media
Fax	Low	High	Rarely	What's a fax?
Smart Phones	Only for voice to voice calls	Use 2 percent of potential	Essential to freedom & flexibility	Is there any other kind?
Twitter	Huh?	Hmmm	Leading	Learning
Blogs	Not Credible Experts	Good Platform	Aggregators	Place to share myself and be known
YouTube	Only when directed there	Growing	Increasing	Learn, Live & Laugh There
Broadcast TV	Authority	Where real reporting happens	TIVO— when and what I can	Screens are everywhere

ATTRACTING NEW CUSTOMERS AND CLIENTS— SELLING TO THE GENERATIONS

All things being equal, prevailing wisdom says people prefer to do business with people they know, like, and trust. When you consider the best way to achieve your goals, it is important to realize that each generation has its own process and gestation cycle of deciding whom it likes and trusts in business. In order to "make the sale," one must be diligent in seeking to understand the Generational CODES that shape the customer's preferred sales style.

GENERATIONAL MOMENTS

Traditionalist Joanne: Joanne, a Traditionalist insurance agent, called to make an appointment to sell me insurance that would cover me and my Millennial administrative assistant. Although it was a small policy, she drove to my office and spent half an hour visiting with us before beginning the business of selling the insurance. She then proceeded to explain all the options and filled out the forms with us and mailed them in personally. My Millennial employee was shocked that she would take that much time for a small client and said, "How can she afford to spend that much time with each person? She'll never make a living that way."

Gen Xer Zack: During a one-day Generationally Savvy Sales Training, a Gen Xer gentleman sitting in the front appeared to be vacillating between puzzled and jazzed. He took copious notes throughout the training, and spent every break in the hall animatedly on the phone. At the end of the day he said, "Thank you; I learned some really good things about Baby Boomers today."

Two weeks later, Gen Xer Zack contacted me to say, "I have something I've got to tell you. I did more business with Baby Boomers in January than I did in all of last year because I realized I've been talking to Boomers like a Gen Xer! I was trying to be respectful of their time by getting right to the facts and business. I thought I was being patient, even though in my mind, I kept thinking, come on, come on, cut to the chase, bottom line it; let's get it done!"

He continued, "After your seminar, I called my Boomer potential clients and asked whether they would like to have lunch or coffee and just spend time together." He laughed as he said, "I never would have thought to do that before. I've been eating ten meals a day, but I've been closing deal after deal because I stopped communicating only like a Gen Xer."

Zack continued, "I finally get it! When I am working to attract Boomer clients, I need to shift into **their** generational style."

What these two stories reflect are two "Generational Moments." Joanne wanted to deliver world-class service that she knew would lead not only to long-term customer satisfaction but also future referrals, and she was willing to invest the time in a small client to build that foundation.

Zack quickly wanted to show that he could offer bottom-line solutions, but he was stepping over the most vital stage of the sale for his Boomer clients, which is to build a strong interpersonal relationship—something Zack typically tries to avoid or at least reserves for people who have demonstrated enough value first.

Generationally Savvy Solution: When you effectively communicate and interact in the generational style of your prospect, you need to spend 90 percent of your time in that person's generational style and only 10 percent in yours.

Traditionalists like to move at a slower, more dignified pace in the timing of their communication and relationship building. The tendency to push to the close quickly and move on to the next pressing task will often shutdown or leave the Traditionalist feeling mistrustful.

A slower pace can be particularly frustrating to Xers and Millennials who want to race ahead once it's clear what is wanted and needed. To push is to lose, especially when a new technology or recently changed system or procedure is the job at hand. At those times, it is most important to slow down and give Traditionalists and Boomers

> TO BE EFFECTIVE IN THE MULTI-GENERATIONAL MARKETPLACE, YOU MUST BE WILLING TO LEARN AND MASTER SHIFTING INTO "SELLING" IN THE GENERATIONAL STYLE OF THE CUSTOMER YOU SEEK TO ATTRACT, GROW, AND RETAIN.

plenty of time to process and incorporate the new procedures and techie tools.

For Baby Boomers, the whole process of selling is about relationships. They love the networking, the bonding, and the schmooze conversations. They enjoy attending charity events, association lunches, and spending time volunteering in high profile places to establish their network of whom they know, like, and trust.

Gen Xers are completely different. Let's read it again, just for emphasis. Gen Xers are different! For those of you who see the value of cultivating the small, but power numbers, of Generation Xers as customers and

> XERS WANT TO GET TO THE BOTTOM-LINE UP FRONT. THEY WANT YOU TO BEGIN WITH VALUE, BE BRIEF AND CONCISE, MAKE A PROMISE, AND THEN, KEEP IT.

clients, read carefully. When you're relating to a Gen Xer, you want to be ready to talk about business opportunities immediately.

It's not advised for you to start a business "get to know you" client call by asking, "So, how are the kids, how was your last vacation, how's the golf game?" For a Gen Xer, the relationship is established by you being an expert as demonstrated through your actions and integrity, not by your title and small talk skills. Xers will volunteer and attend social functions, but only as truly necessary. It's a double bonus if an event advances their professional relationships and supports their children's welfare.

For Millennials in their formative years, the communication tone was positive, upbeat, and friendly. Parents encouraged them to believe in being their best self, speaking up, and sharing their opinions and ideas. They like this tone and receptive attitude.

For Millennials, the attraction/sales cycle is a collaborative one. Yes, they want you to be an expert and find out all about them, but they will also have ideas from the get-go that they expect to be heard and respected and shared through the media they use and love.

When a Millennial is a prospective customer or employee, he will think more of you and your information if you text him to confirm the appointment, hold the first interview via Skype instead of flying him to your location, and present the benefits and answers to many commonly asked questions in an environmentally friendly medium. Killing lots of trees to send them reams of gold embossed paper will not impress a Millennial.

WRITTEN COMMUNICATION—TYPOS, SYNTAX, AND GRAMMAR: OH, MY!

Today, a common area of crisis for managers is the area of written communications: proposals, e-mails, memos, and marketing materials. With the advent of personal digital devices, asynchronous text messaging and instant messaging (IMs), a new shorthand language has been created that is used extensively by Millennials.

Traditionalists and Boomers are caught feeling a little off-balance. They are scrambling to catch up with the technology savvy Gen Xers and Millennial employers/employees, who view the paradigm of technology as the ultimate solution.

Graded on the three R's as children, Traditionalists and Boomers place great value on high proficiency in Reading, Writing, and Arithmetic. Leaders frequently lament that grammar has become a significant and growing issue. Millennials are often so comfortable and proficient with "short-hand" texting that they don't understand the grammar rules or even see the errors in their writing.

Unfortunately, this issue is often hidden or further compounded by the active participation of Boomer parents who review and correct their Millennials' term papers and assignments before their teachers see them. Many parents have extended their support into college and then the workforce by reviewing Millenials' resumes, proposals, pitches, and often sensitive or confidential work product. For the Millennials, it's a bit of a jolt when their Baby Boomer boss is not only unwilling to do the same, but upset that Millenials are exposing the company to security issues.

Generationally Savvy Solution: For leaders with jobs that require strong writing skills, be explicit (not expectant) about writing requirements early on in the interview process. Ask for a writing sample in real-time. (Yes, have the interviewee write an essay in his or her own handwriting during the interview process.) His resume, cover letter, and references have probably all been managed by his parents, and all too often will not be an accurate reflection of a work product you can expect to be delivered by the Millennial alone, but a "mash-up" of the skills of his Boomer parents, teachers, career service professionals, and even personal coaches.

You can complain and get a lot of agreement from other exasperated colleagues, or you can get savvy. One path wastes a lot of time and energy, but you get to be right about how you had it harder in your day. However, you'll still end up frustrated with an employee who makes mistakes you don't think he should.

COMMON GENERATIONAL COMMUNICATION SCHISMS

	TONE	FORMAT	WRITING STYLE
Traditionalists	Stiff—Formal	Snail Mail	Abundant Description
Boomers	Relaxed—Formal	Fax	Data-Centric
Xers	Informal	E-mail	Bullet-Point Concise
Millennials	Casual	Text	Texting Shorthand

ESCALATING CORPORATE "PARENTAL" CONTROL

Proactive and generationally relevant rules about use of social media are absolutely essential for every organization to put in place and review frequently. While many organizations have been escalating the "corporate parental control" functions to manage the flow of communications and block social media outlets, the maxim "That's just how we do it here" is going to be very costly to stand by as companies quickly find that it is dramatically decreasing morale and retention of top talent.

Millennials entering the workforce are coming from a world of being a split second away from updates, insights, and entertainment by their friends, parents, and peers. They walk into your organization expecting to have immediate access and communication with whom they want in the media they favor.

This expectation is causing friction points for many organizations that have protocols and policies that dictate how and with whom you communicate up and down the chain-of-command. In a Pew Research Survey[1] of Millennials in the workplace, 75 percent of Millennials say it's critical to their job satisfaction to have access to social media in the workplace. The point will soon become a mute one since, as personal technology becomes more accessible in pricing, employees will bring their own access. In a follow-up question, respondents shared that if social media outlets are not allowed on their work computers, they will just access them on their personal phones.

Millennials have grown up only knowing communication with the integration of technology. Much of the self-broadcasting and sharing about their lives, friends, and feelings begins at the Millennial HQ, otherwise known globally as "Social Media." Through participating in online communities where information is shared visually, audibly, and in text format, Millennials' home base foundation for their lives is social media.

The expectation that Millennials will go cold-turkey in the office from 24/7 access to friends and family is somewhat akin to expecting every smoker to be able to stop in one day with no problem. The minor difference in this metaphor is that Millennials don't see their reliance on social media interactions as a negative addiction.

COMPROMISE AND CANDOR ARE KEY TO KEEPING MILLENNIALS

In a consulting engagement with a client from a regional professional association, a Boomer manager argued that the amount of time

> "IF YOU'RE NOT TEXTING—YOU ARE THE PROBLEM OF THE FUTURE."
>
> — MILLENNIAL AARON

spent on Facebook and Twitter was negatively affecting productivity so he wondered how to control it. However, upon further exploration, we discovered the team members were meeting all their production goals and productivity, and across the team, productivity was actually up.

Before you take a militant stand on the argument of social media being a drain on productivity, take a closer look at what it's truly costing you and what it could potentially cost you in lost morale and turnover.

CONCLUSION

The key to good communication in the workplace is understanding the preferred communication styles of the different generations and using them to your advantage to communicate. While one generation may not like, understand, or believe in the effectiveness of another generation's preferred communication style, failure to be aware of the differences in styles and to meet one another across generational lines will only result in a breakdown in communication and a lack of productivity in the workplace. When a Gen Xer takes the time to get to know a Baby Boomer, he can sell a product that might not be sold if he just "cuts to the chase." And a Baby Boomer who understands that a Gen Xer views time as precious and wants to "cut to the chase" will be appreciated for not wasting the Gen Xer's time. A middle ground can be found where everyone can flourish in the work environment and feel listened to and appreciated.

6

ORIENTATION

"If you were raised to believe you deserved it all—
is it wrong to want it all?"
— Millennial Jake

SELF-ESTEEM LEVELS BY GENERATION

Traditionalists: As the country slowly began to get back on its feet following the Great Depression, Traditionalists' belief in government and teamwork was fostered as President Franklin D. Roosevelt put their older G.I. siblings to work in national infrastructure projects like the Civilian Conservation Corps (CCC). But just as the horizon looked hopeful once more, the G.I.s and Traditionalists listened to the radio in horror and watched newsreels at the movie theatre showing the European continent being taken over by Hitler's troops. By July 1940, the only free European nation remaining was England.

December 7, 1941 altered the U.S. and the world forever as 183 Japanese carrier-based dive-bombers and fighters attacked the U.S. Naval Base at Pearl Harbor, Hawaii. In his following day address, President Roosevelt captured the essence of a generation's turning point event by declaring it "a date which will live in infamy." Young G.I.s were called to immediate duty and rallied to serve their country with enthusiasm and their HERO archetype "Can do" spirit. The young Traditionalists envied this passion, but they could not participate with their G.I. elders because all but the first few years of their generation were too young to enter the big war as soldiers. They would hear jabs throughout their career from their seniors, "You didn't fight on the front lines. You were a college boy."

Traditionalists became the helpmates and compliant young leaders who planted victory gardens and led the scrap metal drives to support our soldiers. This "missed opportunity" to prove themselves in the heat of real battle would leave them falling into the "Silent" shadow of the G.I.s, earning them a second moniker, the "Silent" generation. Young Traditionalists watched their G.I. dads and older brothers march off to war as their G.I. moms picked up their rivets and entered the workforce to contribute to the cause of defeating evil overseas. But when the soldiers came home, the familiar message of a woman's place being in the home and in the kitchen resounded across America. Family values were a unifying and homogenizing point for Traditionalists. The overprotected children of a Crisis grew up with little breathing room and lots of rules.

Baby Boomers: Following the hard times of financial destitution and a second world war that was fought to protect their freedom, American moms and dads now felt there was no sacrifice too great to ensure their darling little Boomers had every opportunity and chance to make something of themselves. Early childhood development research shows us that when a child feels wanted and appreciated during his or her formative years, a foundation for the rest of life is solidly established to build up the child's psyche. Well, Boomers got that foundation in spades. Doted on as kids, everything Boomers did was in the spotlight, at home, and on the news.

Boomers often felt that the purpose of the world was to serve their needs, wants, and whims, a feeling often carried over into their young adult and midlife stages. Many Boomers still think of themselves as stars of the show and endlessly fascinating. (Yes, you know who you are....) It was a great time to be a kid. Reflecting back, Boomers fondly remember this time as "The Wonder Years."

The optimistic tone and foundation of the High social mood and carefree childhood days gave Baby Boomers the freedom and confidence to speak up and speak out. The country was in a high momentum stage of growth. With increasing stability in many sectors of the economy and world, the children of this social mood rode that wave. Children were encouraged to explore and challenge themselves; the sky was the limit, and the only imaginable obstacle was lack of imagination.

With recent worldwide challenges hovering in their vivid memories, parents now wanted their children to feel everything was solid and safe. Aside from the "duck and cover" bomb drills that found children hiding under their school desks, parents and media succeeded so well that many young Boomers took safety for granted as their birthright. This viewpoint directly shaped their orientation to feel confident, and it gave them the freedom to challenge things without fear in their young adult years of 20-40 (as all Prophet Archetypes do). They launched society into the next Big Shift, the Consciousness Revolution, or the Awakening social mood, known as the '60s and '70s.

Boomers think of themselves as the young vibrant rising energy of the future. Their twenties and thirties were filled with exploration and rebellions both large and small. They took the chant "Never trust anyone over thirty" to heart, and they still see themselves as the force of the future. (Most Boomers, if asked, would say they feel thirty or maybe forty, even if their birth certificate says significantly otherwise.)

The first big wave of business MBA leaders began with the Boomers. They have used their educational advantage to define and refine the use of Corporate Speak, business language, and organizational expectations. While they felt the brunt of "right-sizing," "downsizing," and "recalibrating" in the '70s and '80s, they have come to embrace many of those blanket terms in business today.

Baby Boomers were raised in the culture of feed-on-demand, with Traditionalist parents following the teachings of the beloved Dr. Spock. Their Traditionalist parents were the very beginning Civil Rights leaders. They wanted to make sure that their children would never follow another Hitler, so they encouraged them to think independently, to think about the possibilities.

Gen Xers: By the time the Gen Xers came along, the massive resources that were poured into the starlet babies of the post-war birth boom were now depleted. Schools and organizations built to educate and serve the largest cohort ever born were now crumbling and cracking, badly in need of repairs from the massive wear and tear of the 80 million Boomer children. Instead of repairs and enhancements being scheduled, the small Xer group of 44 million entered schools to be greeted by slashed budgets everywhere. Arts and cultural programs were removed from the curriculum and extracurricular programs were furloughed without a foreseeable return.

As the first generation of latchkey kids, Xers took care of themselves before and after school. They had to deal with processing and understanding the world tragedies that came into their lives through unfiltered access to television. They observed events like Three Mile Island, the Iran hostage crisis, and the terrorist bombings of Flight 103. They were also exposed to leaders putting their own interests before that of their constituents, employees, and families. When after-school programs and financial resources were available, and often they were not, Xers were enrolled in after-school activities until reaching the age of ten or eleven when they were encouraged to begin their independence. Xers' development of self included a strong dose of the messages "Make yourself useful," "Times are tough," and "No one is going to watch out for you."

With not enough child care in their formative years, they lived as exposed children who were constantly seeing the world coming into their home through their TV screen and radio without the interpretation, shielding, or screening of adults. They saw the shadow of Watergate, and the dot-com go dot-bomb. They saw depictions of nuclear war as a likely possibility on television. They were the first children to see a teacher die in the exploration of space through the Challenger disaster.

New dangers to battle were cropping up everywhere for Xers, including AIDS, increasing youth crime, and highly addictive street drugs. Without programs and professionals trained to support them and help process these experiences, Xers often turned their trauma inward with self-directed abusive behaviors such as eating disorders and drugs used not for self-discovery but for self-destruction.

Where Boomer babies had been seen as the promise of the future, Xer children were the first babies whose mothers proudly took "a pill" to try to prevent them. With the rise of two-working parents, a 50 percent divorce rate, joint custody, and legalized abortions, children and nuclear families were no longer in style. More often than not, the family schedules required a complex algorithm to figure out. The concept of sitting down to a family dinner was something that was seen in retro sitcoms but rarely experienced by young Xers firsthand.

On those rare occasions when the nuclear "unit" did gather together, the conversations were not about the Xers' day, friends, or personal challenges. Instead the conversations turned to adult Boomer issues of layoffs or suffering the stupidity of a terrible but tenured boss who clearly demonstrated the Peter Principle in action. Xer children listened and took notes, which included highlights like "If it's to be, it's definitely up to me," "Loyalty is not a two-way street," and "Trust no one." The focus of the world was persistently following the Boomers, and Xers fell in the long cold shadow of their bell curve.

Dangers were not only out on the streets but everywhere for the under-protected Xers. Dangers were being delivered in messages in the media about the scourge of this new generation, from movies featuring devil-child villains as the source of all problems to leading public authorities releasing reports denouncing the Xers as a "rising tide of mediocrity" who were wild and stupid and putting the nation at risk. Generation Xers grew up hearing that they were mediocre, slackers, and, worse yet, that it was their fault the U.S. was falling behind. They are the first generation to be told they would do worse than their parents in every way: money, health, wealth, and educational achievement.

Xers have been the generation to spend the least amount of time with/around adults in their formative years. With both parents in the workforce or living in single-parent households being the norm, Xers became accustomed to being alone and facing and adapting to diverse challenges. But through it all, Xers learned to watch out for themselves as pragmatic realists who created small communities of friends and peers who could be trusted.

As door after door closed in their faces and they were told there was "no room in the inn," or workforce, Xers became the most entrepreneurial generation ever, starting their own businesses and creating products that would shift the paradigms from "withholding information is power" to "sharing information is power."

Our Gen Xers also saw in the '80s massive corporate layoffs and downsizing happen to their parents. Baby Boomers came home and shared their woes, their worries, their frustrations, and their anger at the institutions and organizations. Gen Xers sitting at the table with them listened carefully and told themselves not to trust institutions and organizations. Gen Xers learned that we need to take care of ourselves. There is no one we can rely on but ourselves. "It's up to me if it's to be" became a Gen Xer credo.

Millennials: Here come the Millennials! The prior depictions of children as "spawns of Satan" would completely disappear as the Millennials came onto the scene as the brilliant and brave children saving the world in a style reminiscent of superheroes. With Baby Boomer second-chance families becoming all the rage, abortion rates declined along with divorce rates and the popularity of hands-off parenting. "Baby on Board" signs began to appear not only in mini-vans but also in Lexuses and BMWs, and decal stickers of "My Child is an Honors Student" showed up on bumpers across the country.

As the Unraveling social mood spun faster and faster, national concern to protect and foster children increased with themes like "No Child Left Behind," and new safety protocols such as Amber Alerts and Jessica's Law were put in place to prevent crimes against children. Benign neglect at any level was now a cause for harsh criticism. Politicians and Boomer parents quickly became partners in creating a new kind of "kinderpolitics" full of new rules to protect and promote all things kids. Parents began proudly participating in the day-to-day minute activities of their children's lives.

New technologies that proliferated unchecked in the Xers' childhoods now had new safety features added to create child-safe areas and child-friendly programming and messaging priorities in cable TV, Hollywood, and retail markets. Pop Culture shifted back to wholesome and squeaky clean with the young Miley Cyrus, the Olsen twins, the Jonas Brothers, Purity Rings, the Disney Channel, and Nickelodeon where teams of kids work together to help their parents and authorities make the world a better place. Educators focused on standardized performance, and school uniforms became vogue to promote and equalize the playground. Kids loved being part of their generation again and believed they could do anything and deserved everything.

TEAM—US, ME, I, WE

Generation	Orientation	Motto
Traditionalists	US "U.S."	the greater good—sacrifice
Boomers	Me	personal gratification—explore
Xers	I	the individual—alone
Millennials	We	group power—self-expression

When looking at the world, each generation has a core perspective or "Orientation" that it accesses and fundamentally uses to filter its decisions and through which to interpret events.

Traditionalists: Traditionalists looked at the world and considered how their actions would affect the greater good. The sacrifices they made were made in consideration not just of the individual, but the larger family, tribe, community, and ultimately, the United States (US). Today, you will still find many Traditionalists who only buy American made cars and daily sport the flag pin.

For Traditionalists, the "US" of the group is always more important and outweighs the "me" of the individual, and in fact, they can find it offensive when people think about themselves before the good of the whole. As babies of World War II, they saw the power of pulling together as a team to make the impossible possible. They listened to their older siblings share stories from the front lines of how their foxhole "war buddies" saved their lives through teamwork and discipline.

Boomers: Boomers were the first generation to have the luxury to think about the "ME." Their security and survival were not at risk daily, and they began to look inside and explore who they were and how they could expand on and explore their personal journey to awareness. As they moved from childhood to young adulthood, the social mood shifted with them and launched us into the next Awakening period. Young Boomers were looking for opportunities to find and experience things individually and personally, and they tried a lot of ways (e.g.: sex, drugs, and rock 'n roll) to have the "full" experience of themselves.

If there were an Oscar given for the generation that best played the role of "I love being me!" it would hands down go to the Boomers.

They are quite proud of—in fact shameless about being proud of—being Boomers. Across the country, Boomers will outright ask/state: "We are the best generation, right?"

Not all Boomers explored the world through the Timothy Leary philosophy of "Turn on, tune in, drop out." Many mainstream ways allowed them to stretch the boundaries of personal growth and to live the vow "Never trust anyone over thirty," including by doing such simple things as listening to the radical music of the long-haired Beatles.

As some first-wave young adult Boomers sang about idealistic ways of living to "teach the world to sing," other Boomers moved into midlife by capitalizing on the good life that money offered. New money Yuppies (Young Urban Professionals) and Dinks (Double Income No Kids) embraced and exploited the celebration of "ME" brought to life in the movie *Wall Street*, an archetypal portrayal of 1980s excesses. In the film, the main character Gordon Gekko, a wealthy unscrupulous corporate raider, tells his young protégée, "Greed, for a lack of a better word, is good."

Xers: Our Xers are survivalists. As Nomads who spent the majority of their childhoods alone, or with limited time with adults, each Xer knew, at a fundamental level, "Nobody is looking out for me." The first generation to be accused of putting "A Nation at Risk" by the media and academics, Xers quietly decided, "If anything is going to come out of my life, it's up to me."

Generationally Savvy Solution: Xers care intensely about the greater good. However, their most passionate and loyal support is activated when they see their personal actions today make it safer for their young families' tomorrow. When it comes to engaging adult Gen Xers, leaders are advised to consider how they can make the activity be beneficial for the Gen Xers' Nexter children as well.

Xers will focus on selecting a few charities or deep areas of focus to put their energy. They do not want to over-commit and under-deliver. To enroll and engage Xers on your project or team, create a definitive answer to their question, "How can I personally make a significant, sustainable, and scalable difference?" They will not seek out recognition for their activities and they often resist it when it is offered.

Millennials: Millennials, the "WE" kids, are the first generation of global citizens. They have been happily bubbling in the broth of the melting pot throughout their formative years, seeing the children of many nations represented in their commercials, cartoons, and movies as heroes and allies.

Advanced communication tools have given Millennials a global understanding that there are kids out there just like me who need me. Millennials have been not only pen pals, but they have met in person, Skyped, played video games, and partnered virtually with their peers from around the world in a 24-7 shared community. They proudly speak about what "WE," their peeps, people, peers like and dislike, engaging in the dialogue, "What can WE do to narrow the gap between the HAVES and HAVE NOTS?"

Using this understanding of the different generations' orientations and views of themselves can help business leaders understand how to work with their employees and customers. The globalization of the world economy has not only altered how we think about markets, supply chains, and competition, but has loosened the strangle hold of the nationalistic, tribal paradigm that kept many generations thinking in "U.S." against THEM mode.

Generationally Savvy Solution: Smart marketing executives will leverage this shift in thinking. Global Brands like Nabisco put it in action in their 2010 Beijing Olympics Oreo Cookie ad featuring two Nexter girls from different nations in side-by-side trains. While the Xer moms were busy, the girls discovered each other through the window both classically dunking their OREO cookies in milk. Miming and childish fun ensued as they each instantly made a new friend by recognizing, "She's just like me."

Traditionalists: "How will _____ affect the good of "US—the U.S.," the people of the United States?

Boomers: First generation openly to ask, "What's in it for ME?"

Xers: Learned to ask the question of themselves, "What do *I* need to do to survive?"

Millennials: Demand "What are WE getting out of this deal? Me and my peeps (peeps = non-family members you run with).

RESPECT

The answers to all these generational questions boil down to a very simple principle that is at the heart of who we are as human beings: RESPECT. Everyone wants to be respected for how he or she sees the world. While each generation is unique in its views, they all have two fundamental things in common:

1. They all believe their way of seeing the world is right.

2. They all want respect for how they see the world.

WORK ETHIC—DOES ANYONE HAVE IT?

In a dialogue with two Millennial sales professionals of a global private club organization, I found myself again listening to the most frequently cited major difference between the generations: work ethic. One Millennial team member stated with exasperation, "These kids today just don't know what hard work is and expect everything to be handed to them." By these kids, she was referring to people approximately six to ten years younger than her. I didn't have the heart to tell her that mere hours ago I had heard the same complaint lodged about her coworkers who were her own age with the same fervor.

While each generation complains about the next generation's work ethic, the funny thing is that each generation believes it has a good work ethic of its own. In that case, the critical question really is, "How does each generation measure its work ethic?"

Some generations measure their work ethic in hours, face-time, or line of sight presence. Others pride themselves in getting the work product delivered on time as promised, regardless of how many hours are used, the location, or the time of day they put in the hours. Members of every generation feel willing to work hard to get the job done when they believe in the people and the mission. However, as they enter the workforce, each generation newly tries to push the edge of the envelope and ask new questions regarding what work is:

Work Is...	
Traditionalists	Necessary and my duty to provide for my family
Boomers	The proof of my life accomplishment
Gen Xers	A means to an end
Millenials	Just one aspect of my full life, which should be fun and inspiring

WHAT WORKED FOR YOU IS ONLY THAT—WHAT WORKED FOR YOU!

What worked to entice your generation into a specific organization and motivated you to stay in that organization is not going to be what the next generation cares about at its core. In a 2008 Aplin Recruiting survey of 3,000 workers, entitled "Gen X and Y: What do they want?"[1] the top draw was not a corner office or parking space, but rather the opportunity for growth. Of Millennials surveyed, 96 percent ranked the opportunity for growth as most important, while Gen Xer respondents ranked it as 90 percent.

Let's look now at what is of value and how each generation defines its work ethic.

Traditionalists: For our Traditionalists, their work ethic was driven by a commitment to a legacy. They believed that their children would most likely succeed them in their profession and continue the "family's good name." They worked the hours they were given and were grateful.

Traditionalists' expectations included, "I give you my time; you give me a paycheck." It seemed like a fair exchange. However, they also believed in the implicit contract that the organization for which they worked would watch over them, and watch out for them. Traditionalists wanted to provide food and shelter for their family and education for their kids that went beyond their own. At the end of a twenty-five to thirty-seven-year career well done, they expected no more than a thank you and a gold watch.

Boomers: When Baby Boomers entered the work force in the late 1960s and early '70s, they were optimistic about life and viewed the future as their blank check. They were competitive, driven, and poised to change the world, except they couldn't agree on exactly how. Boomers, like their Traditionalists parents, expected to sign on to a single company for life, perhaps two if a really great opportunity came up. They worked eighty-hour face-time centric work weeks and slowly climbed the corporate ladder, earned their stripes, and did their time in the trenches, confident that loyalty and longevity would be rewarded in the end.

The first generation to say, "Thank God it's Monday," Baby Boomers were driven to establish recognition for their superior performance. A Boomer knew to appear dedicated by getting to the office five minutes before the boss and to stay ten minutes after. They were status-motivated by the goal of getting a corner office, and they were willing to put their personal lives second to achieve the prestigious markers of reserved parking spaces, company cars and five to thirteen-word titles (Senior Regional Vice-President of Global Affairs and Institutional Advancement of Human Capital—WHEW!)

> NO MATTER WHICH GENERATION YOU ARE IN, YOU PROBABLY THINK THE GENERATION THAT COMES AFTER YOU DOESN'T HAVE A GOOD WORK ETHIC.

Gen Xers: Gen Xers' work ethic is based on quietly doing quality work in dedicated and focused periods of time that allow for the most freedom to spend time as they wish and establish security for their families. Gen Xers entered the workforce in the late 1980s with low expectations. They yearned to know that they could enter and stay with the security of one company; instead, they found the labor force already full of the 80M Baby Boomers. The economy was in a recession and openings in the corporate world for the talented Xers were scarce.

Xers adapted by drawing on childhood survival lessons and sought to learn a new skill at each job to make a new bullet point on their portable career resumes. They remain ready for bad news and dramatic changes to happen at any time. They are prepared and feel "If this job or organization fails, or something cataclysmic happens, my resume is packed and ready to go."

Gen Xers watched their Boomer parents play the game of "Corporate Twister." (Right hand on late meeting; left foot on unpaid weekend preparing for the meeting.) Xers took notes as Boomers bitterly complained over the dinner table about how they had to put up with a terrible boss, and backstabbing politics, all sacrifices made in the name of future promotions and promises that went up in smoke, as their parents were laid-off without warning in the recession of the '80s.

Gen Xers' trust of "leaders" and belief in "the rules" went with it. Many leaders are in for an unpleasant surprise. While managers are silently doing succession planning that includes their current bench of Xers, Gen Xers are not planning to move up into management. In fact, most actively resist the pressure to take on any management role, a situation that puts many organizations in a collision course with the leadership gap without a seatbelt or airbag to soften the blow.

Lancaster and Stillman tell us in their book *When Generations Collide* that Xers tend to think about keeping their own careers portable, including leaving the corporate ladder as soon as possible to start their own businesses. One in four Xers dreams of leaving his or her face-time centric corporate gig for a boutique business or entrepreneurship ASAP.

Dear Boomer Parent,

Congratulations! You were amazingly effective in building up your Millennial children's positive self-esteem. You were so convincing, and they believed you. (How were they to know it was just a creative mind-over-matter rhetorical mantra?)

Well, the good news is, "They believed you." And the bad news is "They believed you, and now they work with you."

Corporate America

SCENE: THE COUTURE
CLOSET AT VOGUE.

Rising star Millennial employee Andy Sach is complaining to her Boomer Boss Nigel, "My personal life is hanging by a thread." Nigel responds, "That shit happens when you start doing well at work. Let me know when your whole life goes up in smoke. That means it's time for a promotion."

— THE DEVIL WEARS PRADA

Millennials: As Millennials engage in the workforce, they have high expectations of the welcome they will receive, the options they will have to continue growing, and the opportunities for new and exciting experiences. Millennials want to achieve amazing results quickly, be celebrated for them, and then move on to the next adventure.

Millennials have been the participants and recipients of customized lifestyles from Baby Einstein Learning Programs to Select Soccer Leagues to College and Life Coaches. Their Boomer parents have plotted, policed, pressured, and politically maneuvered their children into schools, internships, and elite programs to create custom experiences for their whole lives.

DON'T ASSUME YOU KNOW THEIR PLAN

The reserved parking space, vacation house, and status of a multi-word title do not have the same Pavlovian effect on Xers or Millennials. Here are two examples:

Gen Xer Alex is the next in line for the CEO position at his international economic development firm. The Baby Boomer CEO is two years away from retirement and the Board of Directors' succession plan includes Xer Alex stepping up. The one small problem is that Alex is planning to leave and start his own consulting firm. He's not interested in taking over the CEO position because it's currently designed to be mostly politics and schmoozing with financial backers. Alex doesn't want to spend his talent navigating politics, so he'll make new plans, unless the Board starts negotiating a new alignment of the accountabilities.

Boomer Bob is perplexed and stunned. A high-level executive at an international banking company, Bob shared,

> **Millennial Rachel** is a Regional Director. She is only thirty and she has reached a level most people never attain, but she just told me her plan to retire is to retire in the next ten years. She is going to have two kids over the next eight years using the company maternity leave and then leave. She's in a position most people from my generation would have killed for, and she is already planning to give it all up!"

THE ENTITLED GENERATION—FACT OR FICTION?
Got Game

In John Beck and Mitchell Wade's book *Got Game: How the Gamer Generation is Reshaping Business Forever* (published by Harvard Business School Press), we see how being a "Gamer" influenced Gen Xers and Millennials' views and consequently affected the way they see business and beyond. Beck and Wade outline the rules and lessons that games are "teaching" Xers and Millennials about "the world." Here is a short sampling:

The WAY IT IS in the Gamer World

The Individual's Role:

- You're the star—you are the center of attention of every game.

- You're the boss—the world is very responsive to your every choice and wish.

- You're the customer, and the customer is always right—the experience is designed for your satisfaction and entertainment; the opponents are tough, but never too tough.

- You're an expert—you have the experience of getting really, really good at something.

- You're a tough guy—you can't be hurt no matter how many crashes and spills you take.

How The World Works:

- There's always an answer—you might be frustrated for a while, but keep trying, it's there.

- Everything is possible—you do amazing things and see other players defeat hundreds of bad guys singlehandedly.

- The world is a logical, human-friendly place—games are basically fair. Events may be random but not inexplicable.

- Trial and error is almost always the best plan—It's the only way to advance in most games.

- Things are unrealistically simple—you can figure a game out completely. Games are built on models. Even complex models can be figured out.

These rules set up the player to feel that high-risk and jumping headlong into uncertainty are the ways to win the game. The more you "die trying" or "crash and burn," the faster you develop mastery.

Along with these new "rules" of engagement and gaming come expectations about what the workplace will be like: diverse, fair, immediately interactive, and welcoming to the new ideas and creations of the newest member on the team. Millennials can master a game in about fifty hours. It seems reasonable to them that they should also be able to master tasks and jobs at work in about the same amount of time. Business leaders looking to attract, grow, and retain younger talent need to ask themselves, "Are we ready and willing to play the game?"

THE FOUR SEASONS LIFESTYLE VS. THE GREAT RECESSION

Coming through their formative years with Baby Boomer parents who had reached a financial high point in their careers, or at least the desire to pretend to their peers that they had financially "arrived," many Millennials had a childhood of first class status. When traveling with their parents, they flew first class, stayed at the Four Seasons in the Private Concierge Suite Level, and purchased only brand name clothing. In their work lives, they expect the same preferential treatment.

Many Millennials did not have their first jobs during their high school and college careers, unless it was for spending money. Their Boomer parents wanted them to focus on their grades and activi-

> MILLENNIALS' WORK ETHIC INCLUDES DOING GOOD WORK IN A JOB WHERE THEY CAN BE SELF-EXPRESSIVE, CREATIVE, AND IMMEDIATELY RECOGNIZED FOR THEIR POTENTIAL AND TALENT.

ties that would make their college resumes competitive, so they gave them allowances and purchased the extras to keep up appearances with the other private school parents.

Let's handle the big question here: "Don't they understand we are recovering from a Great Recession?" For Millennials, the Great Recession meant pushing the PAUSE button on their plans, not the PANIC button. Their Boomer parents blunted the pain by extending the adolescence safety net and welcoming their Millennials home to live in their old rooms with open arms. In fact, they were delighted to have them come home; they missed their best friends. They are proud that their kids like them enough to want to live and hang out with them.

Many Millennials returned or continued on in their educational pursuits to gain an advanced degree. Often, this education was underwritten by Mom and/or Dad taking equity out of the house or not contributing to their own retirement plans to shelter their Millennial from the reality of his or her financial situation. The result is that many of our Boomers are now the working poor, with very little set aside for their own retirements.

RECRUITING—WHO'S INTERVIEWING WHOM?

The vetting process of top talent to choose whom to work for today is a two-way street. Top talent is pro-actively searching out what your company says it is committed to, but even more importantly, how you are fulfilling your promise today.

Gone are the interviews where the recruiter or manager has the exclusive upper hand, and all the information. Now candidates have done their due diligence by:

- Googling
- Surveying their Facebook Friends
- Pinging their LinkedIn Connections with Questions
- Searching the Twitter Hashtag (#) Trends

The interview began long before you even knew they were considering working for you. To attract top talent to you, it's time to put your best image forward as the premier company to join. It's essential that you know what top talent is looking for in an organization. (Not just what you want them to provide for you.)

Your prospective employees will be asking tough questions:

- How does your organization meet my needs and values?

- What opportunities will I have to build my skills here?

- What will my career/portfolio look like in 6, 12, 18 months (not years)?

- What innovative projects/solutions will I work on immediately?

Traditionalists and many Boomers began their careers valuing job security, company history, and job perks such as retirement pensions. By comparison, top Xer and Millennial talent today have motivators lists that include:

- performance-based bonuses

- mobile benefits package (medical being a priority)

- new challenges to learn new technologies

- opportunities to engage in a variety of interesting and diverse projects

- salary integrity (market consistent salary increases)

- meaningful work

- support for my commitment to make a difference

- recognition of my contribution to the big picture

- immediate and frequent feedback

- flexible work hours

- open work spaces and places (telecommuting and virtual teams)

- mentoring and coaching

- a culture of fun and enjoyment of life

- diversity/inclusion of workforce

HIRE SLOW, FIRE FAST

Over three years of judging a competition for the top Forty Leaders in the region under the age of forty, I consistently saw the following core lesson theme expressed by successful leaders, "Take your time in the interviewing process to make sure that your values and expectations match the candidate's. Hire SLOWLY. Be willing to recognize a mistake in judgment quickly and let the individual go QUICKLY."

Generationally Savvy Solutions: Recruiting is for the military. Attracting like-minded team members who align with your values and vision may take more upfront effort, but they pay dividends in the long run. Whether you are an interviewer, a manager, a team member, customer service personnel, or a human resources person, being aware of your and other generations' CODES and blind spots is a vital part of your "recruiting" success.

Deal in reality when seeking to attract new team members. Don't paint the picture you think the candidate wants to hear and think that once you've snagged the person, the battle is won. Employees will call you out on the discrepancies and tell their friends about the situation too—sometimes in a very public way.

It's essential to talent retention that the company evangelists project an accurate reflection of the organization when they seek to convert candidates into employees. It is no longer accepted that if what you were told would be your experience in an organization is not a match for the actual organization, that you will stay. Now, Millennials will leave within the first week, first month, or first quarter if the way the interviewer presented the company does not accurately reflect their early experiences working for it.

You may be surprised what your brand and face to the world are really conveying. Inadequate or poor web presence will ensure that you will not be considered or taken seriously among Millennials and most Gen Xers in the marketplace.

Audit your company website from the candidate's perspective:

- Are you showcasing your values in action, or merely touting them in theory?

- Are all four generations represented in leadership?

- Is the focus on the past history of silver-haired founders or the future talent?

- Do you clearly show the career path a rising star could follow?

- Is job security viewed as a fond memory of times gone by?

- Are pensions and retirement savings plans portable?

Millennials and Gen Xers understand that the coming economy will require technology to be a top priority and they will need up-to-date technology in order for their skills to be effective. They will not want to work for an organization that finds technology to be a second tier priority.

Check your marketing materials for appeal to the generations of candidates and customers you are trying to reach. Regularly hand your marketing pieces to representatives from the four generations and ask for their honest feedback.

FROM SINK OR SWIM TO WELCOME TO THE TEAM

Today, "New Employee Orientation" is out and "Onboarding" is in. New team members need to be welcomed and appropriately shown the ropes, briefed on the ground rules, and woven into the fabric of your organization.

Traditionalists: This generation grew up with a steady guide of trial by fire, and war stories being bandied about where it was a source of pride for the individual to tell how he had survived battle after battle on the job as his way of learning the ropes.

Our Traditionalists started their jobs at a new organization with the philosophy of the senior members being, "Sink or swim! You will either figure it out, or you will be washed out."

Baby Boomers: This generation had the attitude in their onboarding days of "I learned the hard way; so can you. If I tell you too much, then I'm giving you a competitive advantage that I didn't have." With 80 million peers to compete against, Boomers weren't willing to give away this advantage.

Friendly competition is a tone that Baby Boomers have honed to a fine art in business. Their entire formative experience was an ongoing game of musical chairs. Enough resources (chairs) were never available for everyone playing the game. You had to be quick, perhaps throw a few subtle elbows, and keep your seat to stay in the game. For Boomers, the tone of communication is all about subtle competition or outright war with the caveat, "It's just business." Boomers like communications that come across in a positive, upbeat, youthful tone, but they are clear that when push comes to shove, they are still looking out for number one.

Gen Xers: This generation entered the workforce with peer-to-peer latest market information. With the competitive Baby Boomers before them, Generation X's members banded together to help their friends find their ways through organizations. With the advent of the Internet, e-mail could be sent under the radar between the Xers. They helped one another find out the secrets of an organization. They turned the Baby Boomers' theme of "Information is Power, so withhold information to keep the power" on its ear and responded with their own theme of "Sharing Information is Power."

Many Gen Xers didn't have resources invested in them early in their careers. Today they want to see proof that managers trust and value them, and they often equate the amount of training invested in them as proof that the organization is committed to them. Xers feel "The more we learn, the longer we'll stay."

Millennials: When Millenials enter the workforce they expect immediately to be part of the cool action. From day one, they want to like where they work and the people with whom they work. If they don't, during the day they will go onto their social media outlet and update their statuses on Facebook to reflect that they are not having a good time at their new job.

The update will sprinkle out to their community that the job they were so excited about is not turning out as they had hoped. Such information can affect whether peers with similar talents and values in the future want to work at your organization.

WHAT HAPPENED TO 'DO WHAT YOU LOVE?'

Millennials grew up hearing, "Do what you love and love what you do." Now as they enter the workforce, Millennials are shocked to find it surprising to their Boomer bosses that they expect to love their jobs and have fun at work all-day, every day.

An even bigger shock for supervisors and managers is the Millennials' casual expectation that you will be BFFs (best friends forever). (Xer managers are not just surprised by this attitude, but in fact, are so incredulous that they are taking a self-imposed time out to get their emotions under control.)

As our Millennials enter the workforce, it is important to remember that they've been raised on positive coaching from their teachers, their parents, and their protectors.

GENERATIONALLY SAVVY WARNING

Managers beware...Millennials are often surprising in their contradictions; while they have very solid egos, they may lack true self-confidence. Sometimes, they have been protected from experiencing rejection so much that they have very little facility for dealing with it.

After an organization spends so much money to select the right person, it would be criminal to lose that person because the onboarding process was ineffective in helping him to become part of the company and feel like he is part of the team.

Millennials and Xers often have decided in the first week or first month whether they are going to stay with your organization. Certainly within the first ninety days of employment, they have made a decision that could be costly to the organization if they have elected to leave, even if it takes them four, twelve, or eighteen months to find another position before they do leave.

Integrating new people onto the team can always be challenging, but it can also be a rewarding endeavor.

Generationally Savvy Solutions: Generationally Savvy organizations create an onboarding timetable at least thirty to ninety days in duration. The worst scenario is that an organization's management and leaders just neglect new employees because that's the way those older employees were themselves treated.

Putting in place a proactive onboarding program right now can put you ahead of the curve. The easiest way to lose an employee is to make her feel like she made a bad decision by coming to join your company because she isn't able to find her footing or find a way to fit. Avoiding this situation is an easy process if you have the mentoring program to allow somebody to find her place in your culture and immediately feel like part of the team. Millenials are entering the workforce with the expectation that they will be welcomed to your organization in the same way they were welcomed to school, both public and private institutions.

Regularly check and ensure that your company's orientation and training programs take generational diversity into account. Create an immediate mentorship or team experience, something to help new employees feel comfortable and secure from the beginning.

DEVELOPING OPEN CAREER PLANS WITH EMPLOYEES

Leaders are confronting the reality that for Xers and Millennials too, loyalty in the workplace is no longer a two-way street. Partners and shareholders who expect the Generational CODES that surround employment loyalty to be the same for the next generation and match their CODES will be severely disappointed. This Big Mistake has set up many organizations' succession plans for serious breakdowns.

CAREER PLANNING/PATHS	
Traditionalists	20 year plan
Baby Boomers	15 year plan
Gen Xers	5-7 year plan
Millenials	18 months to maybe 3 years

I'M KEEPING MY OPTIONS OPEN

Millennials frequently find themselves bored at work; they begin to fill in their creative needs by creating options through parallel career-pathing. They may be working for your organization, but on the side, many of them are doing small start-up projects. Maybe it's ad hoc temporary work, maybe it's pro bono volunteering, or even a class in a new field, but they are planning another possible career. Often, it's something in the software area or something in the creative area where they have an outlet just in case they're ready some day to step out on their own. They aren't just living one dimension—they're living two or three—and always keeping their options open.

This open-option lifestyle does not seem to them like a breach of contract with their current employers. They understand that if their employers decide they are not needed, the Millennials will be cut from the workforce. So Millennials keeps their options open and a backup plan in play.

Becoming a fully-functioning revenue-producing team member can easily take three, twelve, or even eighteen months from a new hire's start date. But for many Millennials, twelve to eighteen months is about the length of time it takes for them before they will look for a new opportunity or challenge. You can either be open to exploring with them what their futures might look like at your company, or (gulp), if you're not ready to help them find a next step up the corporate ladder or in a direction they want to go with the company, someone from your competition probably is talking to them.

CAREER PATHING: COUNSELOR

Just as corporate America is ready for Xers to move into management, Xers are preparing to step off the corporate ladder and make a little boutique shop of their own.

Whether Xers are partners, stakeholders, or rank and file employees, they dream—in fact yearn—to break out on their own. Approximately one in four Xers plans to start his or her own entrepreneurial endeavor in the next ten years. They are quietly evaluating the value proposition of staying with your organization. Even when they stay in one company for extended periods of time, Xers considers themselves as "Intrepreneurs" (internal entrepreneurs).

The need for employees to have a compatible environment to their Generational CODES is reaching a critical point. Xers may have put up with not having the personal work/life balance they wanted for themselves, but as young families grow, they are not willing to sacrifice time with their kids.

If you want their choice to be to stay with you, you'd better be engaging in active dialogue and negotiations sooner rather than later!

Generationally Savvy Solutions: Millennials are used to having options laid out before them by their helicopter parents and college counselors. Resisting this reality is not a long-term solution. One of the best ways to retain these Millennials is to help them figure out what they want to be "when they grow up." Through open dialogue, managers can discover and address how to capture or channel that creativity and need for expression before it's too late. Remember, if you're not talking to them about it, your competition will be.

Yes, Millennials have high expectations that their career experiences will be personally fulfilling opportunities to make new friends, learn new skills, and connect to a larger purpose. They are looking for a road map to success, and they expect their companies to provide it.

Early in the Millennials' first thirty days, you want to begin the dialogue of their future steps with statements by managers and mentors such as, "We believe it's worth building a career through our company. You are a great match for us and we are putting our investment in you."

"Oh, they want to love their job?" co-workers and leaders may be thinking. "Is that all?"

Millennials, under the intense scrutiny of their helicopter parents, have been working on their résumés practically since they were in diapers. With 76 million peers, Millennials have been competing for spots in daycare, pre-school, and top schools, and now it's time to compete for spots at top companies. They're used to striving to overachieve in sports, academics, and even volunteer services, and now they will want to overachieve on the job for you—if you inspire them.

RETAIN: WHY SHOULD I STAY?

The best companies to work for are consistently articulate not only about the skills employees need to perform well, but they also invest in supporting employees to learn new tools on the job that will add to their portfolios for the future. Although it seems counterintuitive, employers who take an active role in helping employees prepare themselves for the future have lower turnover and higher productivity.

A Traditionalist was happy to have a job at a stable organization where a hard day's work was its own reward.

Baby Boomers lived by the creed that "If I do my job and stay in the game, I will be rewarded with promotions, raises, financial and experiential bonuses, a company car, or other prestige perks like an office position and assigned parking." The system and criteria for evaluation was murky at best, held close to the vest of the top management, and timelines were never clear. It certainly was not acceptable to ask your superior directly, or publicly.

As Gen Xers entered the workplace, they chafed at the lack of communication and asked some bold questions that were ignored until the boom of the dot-com era. Suddenly, interviews were both entrance and exit conversations. Xers were not only asking about their job description and duties, but when their stocks would vest. They asked for transparency in the leadership's exit strategy; alas these conversations did not always go well, and often the Xer was left with broken promises and dashed dreams.

Many Millennials are leaving interviewers flabbergasted by their expectations that employers will have a clear career path lined out for them on how they can quickly move up the leadership success ladder at the organization. They are not willing to wait for someday—maybe if the stars align—to be their career plan. They are demanding that employers have a plan similar to how they selected and completed their major course of studies as undergraduates.

Both Millennials and Xers are looking down the road at what the future holds and how they can prepare for it today. They know that their bosses will make choices that are best for the company and those choices may not necessarily be in their favor.

Generationally Savvy Solution: Have an explicit communication plan that is executed through both your leadership and your literature to engage new team members on Day One, Week One, or Month One.

The optimal career plan includes:

- skills they need to learn, and

- activities and work threads where they can learn them

- timeline by when they can expect to learn the skills through access to cross-training and mentorship

Xers in particular trust employers who invest in them through on-going training on the job and actively solicit their input on designing their future. To begin this process as an employer, ask the team member to:

- Determine clear goals for him- or herself—personally and professionally

- Design a learning plan that addresses the skill sets desired

- Propose a timeline for execution

- Brainstorm the resources needed personally and organizationally to fulfill the plan

BURNT BRIDGES AND SCORCHED EARTH POLICIES ARE PASSÉ

One of the most expensive endeavors for an organization in human capital and pure dollars is the acquisition of top talent. Not only is it tough to find the right candidate, but lateral integration of a new knowledge worker team member can cost an organization $300,000 or more.

Aside from the money spent on researching, reviewing, recruiting, and wooing the new talent, don't forget to factor in the social impact. If the person doesn't integrate well into the company within the first 30-90 days, he will be looking for a new home. It may take him a few months or years, but he will find a match he likes.

OPEN DOOR PHILOSOPHY

Boomers and Traditionalists knew that if they left an organization, the management was most likely saying, "Don't let the door smack your bum on the way out." Today, however, organizations are learning the value of leaving the organization's door open and the bridges intact.

Often times, Millennials want to try new experiences, explore their passions, and even satisfy a volunteering yen. If they don't have the chance to investigate it through your open door/welcome back policy, they will leave you and not come back. But if you have such a policy, they may find the grass is not greener and return to you with new skills and an appreciation for what you provide.

THE ERA OF FREE AGENCY

An overwhelming sense of job insecurity is a daily part of life for employees today. As a result, institutional loyalty as an automatic given is extinct. Instead of the linear progression of past models, business careers may look more like a lattice of moves that include ascents, descents, lateral moves, and holding patterns.

Rather than expecting to start with one company and end with that same company, now Xers and Millenials think as free agents. Being willing to be flexible is not always easy, but according to Deloitte research[2] indicates the benefits of "reduced acquisition and retention costs, increased employee satisfaction and productivity, and greater loyalty through optimal career-life fit" are worth it.

Xers have had plenty of reasons and experiences that told them loyalty is a one-way street—the end of which is a dead end. They saw their Baby Boomer parents having to start over, and they began to learn the lesson that the two-way street of loyalty that their Traditionalist grandparents had talked so much about, and their Boomer parents had touted for years, was no longer there.

Xers understand that there's no reward for loyalty to a corporation. Their loyalty is to an individual, a peer or manager, not an institution. They will follow a good leader from organization to organization. Life employment with a company is not only no longer expected, but in fact, it's rare to find a Gen Xer twenty years into his or her career still at the same organization.

Our Millennials have been creating lifestyle careers. They know the lifestyle they want. While an organization may ask them to be loyal to it, they are clear that it's a one-way relationship.

"ONE SIZE FITS ALL" IS OVER

The one size-fits-all career ladder has run its course. Today's knowledgeable worker is looking to begin a dialogue from Day One/Interview One about the options, avenues, and possibilities he can explore and experience during his tenure at your organization. In fact, the capacity of your leaders, human resource professionals, and recruiters to engage effectively in these conversations directly affects the length of time a top talent will spend with your company.

Organizations that want to attract and retain Xers and Millennials must be willing continuously to match their needs and evolving life circumstances. Many times it will include creating the flexibility for Xers and Millennials to move in and out of organizations or up and down hierarchies as life's priorities and demands shift.

Gen Xer Andrea, a wealth advisor, expressed it this way, "I'm only loyal to this organization for the benefits. I have a young family and the benefits cover them. I could easily go anywhere that offered a competitive package. My husband is an entrepreneur so we are just waiting for his firm to take off and then I will too."

Millenials enter into an organization willing and ready to leave at any time when they don't feel like their employer is providing the appropriate career opportunities needed for them to stay engaged and excited, not bored but always stimulated. For Millennials, providing value is a two-way commitment. Millennials are not just signing on to a company saying, "The only value I expect is my paycheck." They are telling their bosses, "I expect an experience that I am proud to be part of, and satisfied in having given my time and talent to." If Millenials are not feeling opportunities are being presented, they are very likely to jump ship with no sense of guilt, shame, or having left their boss in the lurch.

TWENTY-FIVE YEARS OF EXPERIENCE—ASSET OR DRAWBACK?

Boomers might have thought twenty-plus years of experience was the sign of prestige and loyalty, but Xers and Millennials consider it the sign of stagnation and lack of courage to explore your options.

It used to be that twenty-five years of steady, industry specific experience was the thing that got you credibility. A client frustrated with his search for a new position said to me, "I'm so exasperated. In all my interviews, I'm finding out that they don't think I have the right experience. Don't twenty-five years of experience count for anything anymore?" When Xers and Millennials hear a Boomer or Traditionalist say, "I have twenty-five years experience at this one organization, or twenty-five years experience in this industry or field," they are worried that means they're actually going to have to train, or fight with you on trying new ways and technologies.

Xers are frustrated—okay, ready to tear their hair out—when they hear: "We always did it this way at my last job, and it worked for the last twenty-five years," "We already tried that and it doesn't work here," or "If it ain't broke, don't fix it." Many organizations are struggling with Boomers who feel threatened by the new solutions provided by new media and technology, and who see themselves as part of the last stand to lessen new technology's use so they can remain relevant. For example, one Boomer, while working with a client on a project to engage the Xer and Millennial members' active participation, interrupted a lively brainstorming exchange with a wet blanket declaration, "We've tried all this and it made no difference." However, most of the ideas expressed in the brainstorming session relied on technologies that had only been available to the public for less than a year and were just beginning to be explored for potential use by the organization.

If leaders at the top don't address the dynamics of Boomers blocking the forward progression of technology and flat communication, Xers and Millennials will be taking their skills and passions to a company that will.

Generationally Savvy Solutions: In an interview, when you use twenty-five years as a depth point, it can actually be a detriment, not an asset. Instead, you want to show how you had multiple tasks during your twenty-five year tenure that allowed you to learn new technologies and be open to alternative ways of approaching a problem. Adjust the expression of your experience to illustrate how, while even at the same organization, you were able to:

- lead a number of different projects

- work in a variety of departments

- have diverse experiences of looking at problems with fresh perspectives

CONCLUSION

Companies that want to hire and retain top talent need to get up to speed with the goals and preferences of Gen Xers and Millenials while not letting the viewpoints of Baby Boomers stop the technology's progress and the company's future. The days of loyalty to a company are gone, so companies must understand what their employees want, set clear expectations of employees' job duties, and live up to their promises from day one if they do not want to spend extra time, money, and energy on recruiting, only to lose employees.

7

DISCIPLINE

Following World War II, G.I.s returned from the front and instituted the leadership training and organizational foundation learned in the trenches. Today, many legacy terms and philosophies such as: chain-of-command leadership, officers of the company, all hands meetings, decisions "above my pay grade," and lockstep compensation plans still influence the thinking and expectations of high-level management.

For most of history, generations have been separated in the workplace due to the hierarchical system inherited from the military leadership training and experiences of the G.I./Veteran generation. Work peers entering the workforce were predominantly close in age and generational perspectives.

Today, a leader must adapt his style according to the Generational CODES of the people he is leading. Traditionalists and Boomers are still stunned to be taking orders from someone half their age whom they quietly mutter is still wet behind the ears.

It goes all the way to the top as evidenced in a June 27, 2011 *Newsweek* interview with retiring Pentagon boss Robert Gates when he said, "Hillary [Clinton] and I call ourselves the Old Folks Caucus....

And I must say, it's the first time in my life I've worked for a president who was 20 years younger than I was."

Traditionalists: Traditionalists believed in the promises of big institutions and organizations. The golden horizon was that one day you would have the seniority, and then it would be your turn to be the boss, call the shots, lead the troops. In the meantime, you gave your best, and waited with the expectation that eventually, the best would be returned to you.

For Traditionalists a "healthy" fear of the boss/commanding officer was considered wise. It was understood that moving forward was directly correlated to staying on the boss's good side and making the boss look good. Traditionalists obeyed the chain of command and "dug in" to their place in the organization's hierarchy. They followed the rules of the day and became "company men," and for the most part, their expectations were met.

Times have changed.

Baby Boomers: Baby Boomers flooded the workforce with high hopes for the world and even higher expectations of changing the way work was done. With their secure childhood during the rise of productivity and growth in the High social mood behind them, young Boomers entered the workforce ready to challenge the authority and question "the man." As young adults of the Consciousness Revolution, Boomers advocated turning the traditional corporate hierarchy upside down.

Although Boomers may not like to remember it this way, they were considered very difficult to manage, and their entry into the workforce was not met with huge upticks in productivity. Why? They were arguing with everyone about everything, and if they weren't happy about how they were being treated, they encouraged their peers to argue as well.

G.I. and Traditionalist bosses saw their questioning and challenging attitudes as rude, entitled, difficult to manage, and oh yes, lacking in strong work ethic. Sound familiar?

Boomers were genuinely passionate about bringing fun and spirit into the workplace, but the reality fell a little short of the big goal. While Boomers read, talked, and shared their ideas and theories of egalitarian leadership and participative management, with 80 million peers/competitors, Baby Boomers quickly began learning the rules of the game and how to work the system. Non-Boomers who work for a Boomer Boss will tell you that their boss's career habits, formed from working for command-and-control Traditionalists and G.I.s, are often still very much in evidence.

Gen Xers: With the boom of the 1970s ending with the bust of the '80s recession, Gen Xers watched their parents scrape and scrap to climb the corporate ladder while hating their bosses, leaders, and jobs, but still basing their self-worth on the awards and recognition delivered by those same people and institutions. Xers saw their parent(s) work twenty-hour days and give up "quality time" with their family to work late and impress the boss.

Xers' innocence was stripped away when hard times hit and their parents were cut loose without warning in the prevailing economic recession winds of "down-sizing and right-sizing" for the company's benefit.

Consequently, Xers are suspicious of all "corporate speak." While prior generations believed in the companies that made social contracts with employees, such as, "You work hard for us, and we'll take care of you," Xers know firsthand that the corporate vision, mission, and values are generally only aspirational at best, and more accurately, would be found under the genre of science-fiction or fantasy.

Xers feel like they are in a never-ending search to find a (work)place to call home and leaders whom they can trust and believe. Along with broken promises in the workplace, Xers experienced up close the moral bankruptcy of leaders at every level of private and public institutions.

Observing the first Presidential resignation in U.S. history just as they were beginning to become politically aware fundamentally shaped their beliefs in the lack of sanctity in public servants. From Exxon spills to Enron chills, Xers may have hoped for the best, but their core survivor mentality kept telling them to prepare for the worst just when they thought it was "safe to get back in the water." (Duh Dunt, Duh Dunt—Imagine scary *Jaws* music playing in the background. Xers do.)

Millennials: Millennials respect authority, but they do not fear it. Millennials had formative years filled with fans, friends, coaches, cheerleaders, and BFFs (Best Friend Forever). With Boomer parents wearing the BFF status as a medal of accomplishment, Millennials were encouraged to call their parents by their first names from birth and their grandparents by nicknames (Nana, Pop Pop). Consequently, Millennials have a very casual relationship with elders and authority figures.

Parents knew what they should do, but the threat of their children not liking them, or making a public scene was enough to dissuade them from pushing the issue. From the time they were in diapers to texting at the dinner table, Millennials prevailed every time they challenged their Boomer parents. Boomers' commitment to being "liked" by their children meant removing the implementation of penalties or consequences for disobeying the leader/parent.

No longer do we have the unquestioning, follow-the-rules Traditionalists in charge; now authoritarians are on trial. Boomers parents have organized the PTA into a significant political entity to fight collectively and individually on behalf of their Millennials when authoritative figures, such as teachers, attempt to discipline or punish their children.

OLD MODEL	NEW MODEL
Manager	Coach
Superior	Peer
Boss	Partner

AM I THE BOSS OR THEIR BFF?: WHAT'S PARENTING GOT TO DO WITH IT?

Traditionalists: For Traditionalists, having a 1950s television *Father Knows Best* nuclear family image firmly in place and the capacity to provide for the family's basic needs was a sign of success. A large family was admired as a sign of prosperity and virility, and your children's behavior as upstanding citizens who followed the rules directly reflected upon your reputation.

While parents were still strict, especially G.I. parents who believed in the "spare the rod and spoil the child" adage, after surviving the horrors of World War II, Traditionalists also wanted to make sure their children were independent thinkers and would never follow the likes of Hitler or Stalin.

Traditionalists raised their Boomer children with a new philosophy influenced by the much-loved Dr. Spock who told them to nurture their children. Boomers were given the widest latitude of any generation thus far to grow and challenge boundaries. Traditionalists encouraged their Baby Boomer children to run, play, and explore big ideas.

Baby Boomers: Baby Boomers were the new possibility and darlings of the post-war High period. They were the hope of the bright future;

however, many early Boomers found themselves in a position of conflicting priorities.

Boomers were encouraged to attend college and start young families, while simultaneously launching new careers in a highly competitive labor market. Boomers wanted to explore the pleasures and riches available in the rise up the corporate ladder, but they had young Xer children dragging on their freedom.

For many Boomers, the call of their careers and exploits overrode the needs of their own children and spouses, leading to second and third marriages and families. As "do-over" parents with second families and sometimes third families, Boomers doing "Family Part II" often went to great expense to have their Millennial child i.e. in-vitro, surrogacy, and/or adoption. Boomers are determined to do parenting right this time, which includes being BFFs with this crop of Millennial children.

Gen Xers: Xers grew up in a "parenting by proxy" world surviving one dysfunctional family situation after another. With step-siblings, half-siblings, and the "yours, mine, and ours," Xers' "family of origin" reality was often fragmented at best.

Xers have been seeking a sense of authentic-family their whole lives. In a time when the nuclear family model was still held up as the right way to grow-up, being from a broken family created a stain on the reputation of both the parents and children.

Although, skepticism and disappointments were their constant companions, Xers still cobbled together makeshift "family of choice" solutions. Xers' parents didn't attend every sporting practice, or even the big game, recital or debate; instead, it was their peers who were there for them. They turned to their friends and fellow Xers for comfort, support, and a sense of family.

This mindset can be seen depicted in the popular 1990s television series *Friends*, which shows us how a young group of Xers banded together to live the promise of the show's theme song, "I'll Be There for You" as they attempted to negotiate through life, work, and courtship rituals. For Xers, peers were/are the most trusted and important part of their lives, until they start having their own children.

As they move up and on in their careers and life stage, we see the second stage of the "family of choice" in action with *Grey's Anatomy's* Xers starting their surgical internship at Seattle Grace. The main character, Xer Meredith Grey, deals with the demons of being the neglected child of brilliant Baby Boomer surgeon, Ellis Grey. Grey's mother made her career top priority, and her romantic affair came in as a close second, leaving her family and her Xer child to fall into distant last place, an afterthought.

As the series progresses, each Gen Xer character's story of childhood survival is revealed to us from Izzy Stevens' dizzy, hippie mom who can't handle life's tough spots to Alex Karev, who was abandoned and grew up in foster homes where he cobbled together a makeshift family he still supports.

A very telling family-of-choice moment comes when character Christina Wang needs surgery and must fill-in her emergency contact information on a form. A poster-child for Xer loner/individualism, Christina admits to Meredith that she feels they have become family by saying, "You're my person." For Xers, true family has little to do with blood and a lot to do with whom you can call "my person," the one I want called in case of emergency.

COMPETING WITH GEN XERS' CHILDREN FOR THEIR TIME IS A SLIPPERY SLOPE

It is imperative for leaders to realize that for Xers real "quality time" with their offspring trumps all other commitments. Spouses are important, but children are the ultimate. Xers' belief in the longevity of relationships is still mixed with a healthy skepticism left over from the failure of their parents' relationships.

When you ask Xers to commit their time from 3-9 p.m. on weekdays or anytime on weekends, you are directly competing with their precious babies. While many Boomers still feel that time is less valuable than the money work can put in their pocket, time is priceless to Xers.

If you are asking a Gen Xer to do something that does not support or advance his or her kids' current or future success and wellbeing, you have a tough fight ahead. Making policies, projects, or programs that prevent Xers from watching their children's little league games, swim meets, or piano recitals will create a friction point that can ultimately be a deciding factor in Xers leaving your organization.

Xers' absorption in their children's lives can be puzzling for others until they realize the sense of purpose many are finding in the journey of parenthood. A classic example, early Xer Johnny Depp declares he was saved from self-destructing by his children. The former hell-raiser, renowned for drinking heavily, trashing hotel rooms, and scrapes with the paparazzi, claims becoming a father put a stop to his wild ways and fruitless search for meaning. In an interview for his 2010 movie *The Tourist*, Depp told Britain's *Daily Mirror* that being a dad is the "only thing I want to be good at in my life. I worship my kids and I learn from my kids."[1]

Xer parents are clear about their roles. Dan, CEO of a securities firm, expressed the Xer philosophy well by saying, "We are their parent first and their friend second. We provide boundaries, rules and make sure there are consequences for negative actions, but we do it with lots of love, and always make it clear we adore them."

TREND—STAY-AT-HOME-PARENTS

A key trend impacting the talent pool is the Gen Xers' choice to have one stay-at-home parent. Xers are opening new horizons and giving themselves permission to stop living the double-barrel corporate couple life. Their kids are the top priority, even if it means one of the parents opting out of work for a few years. No more is it just the stay-at-home mom; now the Xers are deciding which parent's earnings can best support the family and which parent can stay home.

Organizations need to make sure they have equal paternity and maternity policies and philosophies in place to address the increasing demands. Even if a couple does not choose to have one parent stay home, Xers are looking for flexible schedules and control of their time. They are committed to delivering high quality work products, but they want to be free to make work fit in with their family priorities.

Xers' emotional scars from weekend fathers and visitation schedules run deep. They are going to hold onto marriages as long as they can and make sure their children feel wanted and safe, even if it means passing up a promotion or pay raise to do so. To have the power to be present and energetic with their kids is a sign that they have power in and over their own lives.

HELICOPTER PARENTS—AKA BLACK HAWK PARENTS

Chances are you have heard the term "Helicopter Parent" and thought that it applied only to the extreme edges of the Boomer parents. When I first bring this term up in my keynotes and trainings, I often hear embarrassed chuckles from the audience and see a few blank looks that I imagine reflect the thought, "Who would do such a thing? Certainly not me."

However, as I describe the actions of helicopter parents, recognition dawns in the audience members' eyes, and people start to be a little bit less confident that it does not apply to them.

Here are a couple of tests to see whether you know someone who is Helicopter Parenting (perhaps even you):

- You grammatically corrected your children's papers in grade school, high school, college, and/or resume and even their work products after they entered the work force.

- You reminded your children repeatedly about dentist, doctor, sports, musical or other appointments starting three weeks out, two weeks out, one week out, and then every day of the week prior to the appointment to make sure they would not forget it.

- You called to follow up with your children's teachers about their homework and whether your children were turning it in.

- When your child had a problem at school, you called the high school or college to find out what could be done about this problem versus having your child figure it out for him- or herself.

- When you sent your child to summer camp, you called daily to make sure your child was not lonely and tried to smuggle in a cell phone so he or she could call you.

- When you haven't received a call or text once a day at minimum, you begin to worry that your child doesn't love you anymore, or that something has happened to him or her.

- You've visited your child on-site at his job and have met his boss and work friends.

- You asked to be your child's friend on Facebook.

- You hired a personal coach for your child while she was still in high school to help her get into college.

- You consistently text your child more than five times a day just to check-in and see how/what she is doing.

- You actively learn your children's texting lingo and know how to use properly: LOL, K, CU, BRB.

- You attended every sporting event and practice throughout every sport season.

- You requested the college informational brochure and application for your child.

- You filled out your child's college application.

- All the above

GENERATIONALLY SAVVY WARNING

It's not just a U.S. phenomenon—it's global. In Sweden, what the U.S. calls helicopter parents are called Curling Parents, in reference to the sport of curling where an individual slides a stone down an ice path. Two other people get in front of it and brush away all of the rocks, stones, or anything else that could possibly create friction even going so far as to melt the ice to allow an even easier and more directed glide to slide into the spot the brushers (or parents) see as optimal. These kinds of parents, who remove every obstacle away from their Millennial children, have been made famous for a parenting style that includes heaping praise and plenty of hovering over their children's critical thinking decisions to help them avoid pitfalls, remove obstacles, and achieve success.

Millenial Grace and Baby Boomer Tom Go to College

A Baby Boomer client, let's call him Tom, was taking his Millennial daughter, Grace, to her first year at a private college. For weeks, they had been buying and preparing for the perfect college experience by texting back and forth dozens of times a day. On the big day, Boomer Tom helped Millennial Grace move into her dorm room, buy her books, run to Wal-Mart for treats and sundries, and get settled.

Finally, it was time to say goodbye. Boomer Tom was finding it very difficult to leave, but Millennial Grace was excited. As Boomer Tom arrived at his hotel, he tearfully texted words of love and encouragement to Millennial Grace.

A few hours later, Millennial Grace had not responded to his texts. Boomer Tom was bummed but not worried. He continued to text Millennial Grace throughout the evening and into the next morning.

By 10:00 a.m., Boomer Tom was a mess. Millennial Grace hadn't responded to any of his text messages or voicemails for seventeen hours. Didn't she need him anymore? Had she already replaced him? Was she hurt? It was less than a twenty-four hour period, but already Boomer Tom's propellers were revving up to go in for search and rescue, which of course was unnecessary since Millennial Grace was fine and just immersed in orientation fun and bonding.

For Xers, the Millennial who expects them to hover over every aspect of their lives and work, based on their parenting experiences, is in for a rude awakening. Xers' memory of starting college is a little different. They arrived with two suitcases and a warning to stay out of trouble.

THE PARENT FACTOR

Remember when "Bring Your Child to Work Day" was all the rage? Now that those children who were brought to work are in the work force themselves, they are turning around and extending the favor to their parents. *The Wall Street Journal* writer Ron Alsop reports in his book *The Trophy Kids Grow Up* that today organizations are taking the opportunity to create a new classic, "Bring Your Parents to Work Day."

Choosing a new company to work for has become a meta-level, and meta-meta-level decision-making process, or said another way, it's complicated, and yes, it will involve Millennials and, like it or not, their parents. The bonus factor is if you work with the parents, they can be part of the sticky factor in your favor when their Millennial calls home for advice when the going gets tough. Let's look at an example:

Millenial Nick

Millennial Nick was frustrated with his boss, office politics, and being "low man on the totem pole." He called home to vent and get support for his decision to quit. Nick was surprised to hear his mom stand up for his boss. Nick says, "She pointed out how some of the things my boss had shared during orientation were similar to what I was mad about. I decided to give it another try."

Businesses who want to recruit top talent have to understand how to follow what private high schools and universities have already done to compete for the top student who has high expectations and standards for custom communication.

Schools have dedicated follow-up channels and specific promotional materials, including brochures, website pages, and blogs to address exclusively the questions, concerns, and activities of parents.

Generationally Savvy Solutions: Remember the Gamers' mentality? Gen Xers and Millenials are looking for a strategy to help them figure out the game of business and how to get to the final goal or win the game the quickest. They look for leaders who will provide a meta-map of the organization and strategic thinking on how to plan their careers to be successful as fast as possible.

When you are seeking to recruit and attract people to your organization, make sure you use the multiple channels your prospective talent is using. When Xers and Millennials investigate an organization, the first thing they research are the public, visual, digital, and social media discourse cues that tell them:

- Who is really running the company?

- What do you truly value by directing resources to it?

- How diverse is your leadership

- Are you truly inclusive about how you listen and advance your talent?

You may be telling prospective employees that you are a forward thinking, innovative, and open organization, so they will feel right at home in your egalitarian decision-making culture, but that belief does not show up anywhere except in theory. The points of truth Xers and Millennials use to validate what you say with what you do may contradict you.

A website that opens brandishing language about one hundred years of tradition and showcases a line-up of silver-haired, white men over sixty as the leading thinkers of the organization does not engender the thought, "Wow, I belong with these people." What it may communicate, however, is that while you may need young talent, the old guard still pulls the strings.

An example of how organizations are trying to create parent-friendly communications and experiences to attract Millenials and their Helicopter parents comes from the U.S. Armed Services. Boomer parents, whose formative experiences included protesting the deployment of troops to Vietnam, were not entirely receptive to their Hero archetype Millennial children's desire to join the military. Consequently, in 2010 the Army launched a video ad series focused on how to sit your parents down to discuss that you want to enlist in the Army.

Here are guidelines to designing an attractive perception of your organization and turning it into reality:

1. When designing your attraction communications pipeline develop two lines in your plan:

   - One line that goes directly to the Millennial worker.

   - A second line that goes directly to the Baby Boomer parent. It can have a more reduced level of information but address the commonly asked questions.

When a Millennial begins interviewing at your company, proactively ask him whether he would like someone in his life to receive the second stream of communication.

2. Invite parents of Millennials to attend an onboarding program with a special set of programs just for them. Remember, college orientations are the frame of reference for helicopter parents. Universities take full advantage by creating an entire weekend designed to help familiarize the student and the parent with the institution, decrease anxiety over a myriad of normal, but new experiences, and engage everyone in feeling institutional ownership.

3. Develop an official "Bring your Parents to Work Day." Boomer parents are going to sneak in any way to see where their Millennial children work, so you may as well design the experience to be one that puts you in the driver's seat. Include time to have parents meet their Millennial's boss whom they have been hearing so much about.

SHOULD I STAY OR SHOULD I GO NOW?

The number one reason people have consistently reported for leaving an organization, regardless of their generation is...drum roll please... they don't feel appreciated. It may come out sounding like, "I don't get paid enough to put up with this!" or "I've got a better offer elsewhere." But at the core of exit interviews and one-on-one dialogues, the basic message is that they didn't feel like their contribution was recognized.

This sentiment and dilemma is only going to increase as the percentage of Millennials continues to increase in the workplace.

Feedback—The Golden Skill of Leaders

One of the most important and vital tools of leadership is the capacity to deliver authentic and **frequent** feedback in a way that matches the Generational CODES of a team member, colleague, or customer.

The expectations of the workplace experience have fundamentally changed over the last fifty post-World War II years as we have moved out of the lower stages of Maslow's hierarchy of survival, shelter, and food and into the higher levels of self-actualization and self-expression. Managers who attend my workshops will often say with exasperation, "I don't understand what their (people in a younger generation) problem is! They are getting paid for what they do. What more do they expect?"

Rob, a Boomer client in technology, exasperatedly shared, "I actually state explicitly in the first interview, 'I want people who will give me a day's work for a day's pay. Are you up for that?'"

Actually, today employees expect a lot more. No longer are "workers" satisfied with the equation of working for a paycheck as an equal trade. If they are spending the majority of their waking hours contributing to building your business and advancing the company's goals, they want to be considered team members, not employees, and recognized for their part in creating a successful outcome.

Yes, Traditionalists and Baby Boomers, I hear you reading this and mumbling to yourself, "I came up through the ranks without being acknowledged for just doing my job. Getting a paycheck was acknowledgment enough!" But if you continue to say that, you will watch a lot of talented leaders and managers walk out your doors.

READY OR NOT, IT'S TIME TO TURN IT UP: FEEDBACK IN THE WORKPLACE

As you read through this section, it might make it easier to think of how you'd treat your kids, nieces or nephews if they were working for you and asking for advice and feedback. Remember your own precious Millennial offspring is right now an employee of another Boomer, Xer, or Traditionalist, and probably driving the employer a little bonkers. Let's look at how each generation likes to receive feedback in the workplace.

Traditionalists: For our Traditionalists, turning up the feedback could be a little painful. For the most part, our Traditionalists' philosophy comes right out of the G.I. Generation's military model of leadership where "No news is good news." My father's favorite saying was, "If I'm not yelling, you're not in trouble."

Baby Boomers: As the Baby Boomers entered the workforce, this "no news" approach wasn't quite enough information. They had 80M peers/competitors with whom they were locked into a gladiator-style battle, and they were looking for a little more data on how they were doing. Boomers thought it was a huge success when they got the annual review instituted. Once a year, they sat down in a very formal, structured environment and learned from a manager armed with lots of documentation, stats, and data how they stacked up against their peers as well as their managers' expectations.

Gen Xers: This generation's members definitely appreciate the bottom-line of facts and data, but given their latchkey childhood, the limited amount of time with adults in their formative years, and the lack of mentorship support early in their careers, Xers can feel a little neurotic about their professional performance. So they will say, "Once a year is not quite enough."

Xers prefer to have immediate feedback tied directly to their performance. Xers see right through phoniness and it grates on their nerves like a personal attack. A common scenario for a great Xer feedback moment is right after a meeting where the Xer presented a pitch. Immediately, the Xer might stop his Boomer boss and say, "Excuse me; I'm sorry to interrupt, but how did I do in that meeting?" The Boomer boss may respond, "Whoa, whoa, whoa, give me some time to collect my thoughts and write them down. Let's do this right. I want to be sitting in an office at a formal desk with you on the other side of the desk."

Meanwhile, the Xer is saying, "It doesn't have to be formal or final; just give me your impressions, off the cuff, from the gut, but be honest with me. None of that, you know, corporate speak, or fluffy stuff. I want you to be straight. How I am doing?" For Xers, the more you make feedback vivid—specific with no puffery and no fluff—the better.

If you are beginning to get uncomfortable and think you can never keep up with all these feedback needs, brace yourself for the Millennials.

Millennials: Millennials' parents gently corrected them through "teachable moments" when they needed it, but praised and cheered for them at all other times. New language designed to support the development of their Millennials' self-esteem focused on enhancing performance through upbeat messaging. Millennials' parents and teachers encouraged them to shoot for the stars and give it their best. Instead of referring to their performance as making errors or mistakes, parents and teachers didn't tell Millenials they got the answer wrong; rather, they said, "You almost got it right, and this is what you can do to make it better (or more right)." The result of this focus on Millenials' self-esteem, can result in situations like the following one in the workplace:

Millennial Tricia

A Gen Xer friend called me one day in a confused and exasperated state. As the president of a mid-sized PR firm, she was proud of leading the organization through a growth phase that resulted in the firm being recognized as one of "Fastest Growing Companies and Best Companies to Work For" in the region. She was shocked, however, one day to be confronted by Tricia, a Millennial intern asking her, "Why don't you like me?" The Gen Xer president replied, "What do you mean?" Tricia proceeded angrily to assert that the Gen Xer President had not acknowledged her publicly for anything she had done exceptionally well in over two weeks. The Gen Xer said, "We just did a review last month." Millennial Tricia responded, "Yes, but that was a month ago. How am I supposed to know how I'm doing now?"

When Millennials do not receive what they feel to be sufficient feedback, they feel a little bit like they are playing a game of "Blind Man's Bluff" where they have been blindfolded, led into the workforce, and asked to perform a task without sufficient information. They are used to feeling their way forward, but without the verbal feedback of people they respect and admire, they are casting about, drifting about, wandering about without clarity on what's next. Their steps become faltering. They reach out and feel unstable and shaky. They need to receive cues and directions on how they are doing. Otherwise, they are completely disoriented in your workplace. Just remember, it needs to begin with what they did right!

Johnson and Johnson in their book *Generations Inc.* assert that Millenials' behavior is not as predictable as we may desire, "You cannot assume that their parents or school prepared them to understand what your expectations will be on the job for performance and attitude."

Feedback Guide for the Generations

Traditionalist	No news is good news
Baby Boomer	Formal annual reviews
Gen Xer	Immediate, authentic, applicable
Millennial	Frequent, positive, coaching

Generationally Savvy Solution: MORE—LESS—KEEP: The first place to begin addressing the need of Millenials for more feedback is to focus on the tone, frequency, and style you deliver needed ongoing feedback. The operative word in the previous sentence is "ongoing." I know that providing ongoing feedback can be a source of frustration for many Traditionalist and Baby Boomer leaders as well as some Xers, but more feedback is needed than you are probably currently comfortable giving.

Training your leaders from the top down and the bottom up can be done through a simple practice called "More-Less-Keep."

The basic framework of this practice is to start with **MORE**: what the team member is doing right. (Most of us respond best when we hear an authentic reflection of what we have done well, so this works for more than just Millennials.) You need to reflect on where the employee is already being successful or productive and let him know you want him to do MORE of the same in those areas.

Next, you move to **LESS**: the area where the employee needs performance improvement or correction. Here you give constructive advice on what you want the employee to do LESS of or stop doing altogether.

You finish up the interaction with **KEEP**: something that is working well exactly at the employee's pace and how he or she is currently executing it.

BONUS: This process works well for Boomers and Xers too! Everyone likes to hear the positive, yet 65 percent of employees report never hearing positive feedback in the workplace.

As simple as this method is, it's not easy for many managers and leaders to retrain themselves. Often, managers want to go directly to what doesn't work and stay there. For Millennials, specifically, this focus is abrasive and often shuts them down entirely from hearing the constructive side. Instead, they hear "You don't like me."

TO GIVE A TROPHY OR NOT TO GIVE A TROPHY

One of the most important and vital tools of leadership is the capacity to deliver authentic and frequent feedback in a way that matches the Generational CODES of a team member, colleague, or customer.

Managers who attend my workshops will often say with exasperation, "I don't understand what their (people in a younger generation) problem is! They are getting paid for what they do. What more do they expect?"

One popular and sticky moniker for Millennials is the "Trophy Generation." Millennials were raised hearing the coaching, "Just do your best." Baby Boomers wanted their children to have high self-esteem, so they made sure that their Millennials did not feel left out.

The soundtrack to the movie of the Millennials' childhood has been filled with a steady diet of constant kudos and positive messages praising everything they did or every effort made. Baby Boomers were the first generation who embraced pop psychology and the philosophy of "I'm okay, you're okay; I'm just so proud of you for trying." Millennials have been given credit for just showing up—not for getting the job done or even winning, just for showing up.

Now, before you become righteous and say to yourself, "I can't believe these kids today!" ask yourself: How many times have you attended a grade school or high school sports banquet, whether it was soccer, baseball, or football, and everyone received a trophy? Not just a trophy awarded to the MVP or the captain, but EVERYONE got a trophy for participating.

Again, there's a little twist to consider in this situation. While the Millennials are the ones going home with the shiny trophies, or blue ribbons, who bought the trophies? Yep, their Baby Boomer parents, not wanting their children to feel bad or left out, bought enough trophies for everyone.

Gen Xers, you might be feeling a little self-righteous about now, but don't be too smug. You're Nexter child had a full graduation ceremony from kindergarten with mortar board and gown.

"LEAD, FOLLOW, OR GET OUT OF THE WAY" IS SO YESTERDAY

Presenting the authoritarian model of leadership as the path to success is a turn-off to Xers and Millennials alike that will keep them from even entering into your candidate pool. Lockstep compensation based on earning your stripes in the trenches over time smacks of hierarchical favoritism.

Today, talent wants to see examples of how and where you put your values in action. When you say you value innovation, how do you execute on that statement?

Baby Boomers may have tolerated occasional meetings and annual performance reviews with their bosses, but Millennials are expecting and actually craving frequent contact with their bosses.

The backlash in the workplace today shows up when a Boomer-coached Millennial walks into your office with confidence and high expectations of being recognized immediately for his terrific potential and unrealized talent on Day One.

When Millenials attempt, try, or participate in a project and they don't hear the expected "atta-girl/boy," they are going to think you don't like them. And you know what they are going to do if they think you don't like them. They're going to begin to plan their exit strategy to leave, and you many never know it. Can you afford to have people leave just because they didn't feel like you saw their potential or appreciated what they did?

For Millennials there is an expectation of liking the boss, receiving lots of praise for their performance, and maintaining an open exchange of ideas where their opinions and concerns are taken seriously.

Millennials want their bosses to be their BFFs and their coaches. Their parents, teachers, and coaches have all given them positive reinforcement for at least giving it a try regardless of the level of success. Understand that even when they got a task wrong as a young one, they were not told it was WRONG. Instead they were told, "You made a really good effort, and we're proud of you for that. It's almost right. Here's what you can do to make it all the way right."

A client shared the story of a young, new associate, who asked a senior partner at a law firm to review a document that had just barely begun to take shape. Since the document was in the first stages, the senior partner was offended that the young person would be so informal. He told him to come back when he had a complete draft. The Millenials' response was, "Why should I keep working on it until I know I'm going in the right direction from the beginning?"

LAPEL PINS, SECRET HANDSHAKES, PASSWORDS, AND PROTOCOL

Despite the entrepreneurial heritage of the U.S., for the G.I. Generation, Traditionalists, and Boomers, your family name and legacy could still open or close doors, so building a reputation was a multi-generational endeavor. Today, however, Gen Xers and Millennials are measuring the value of membership in companies, associations, and non-profit organizations with a new yardstick.

Exclusive membership into private clubs, societies, and fraternities has long been a carrot to dangle in front of the ambitious and talented. The time, energy, and resources required to establish the network, value propositions, and elite status of membership were daunting. But today, the combo of technology and talent can give Xers and

Millennials tools to level the playing field, to network socially, and to create their own groups.

As declining membership in professional associations, traditional service organizations, and fraternal clubs reaches crisis proportions, many Traditionalist and Boomer members are nervous, frustrated, and puzzled. The question that rolls around is, "How do we get more young members involved?" A valid question, but the answer requires a willingness to be open to change.

Many times, clients in both the for-profit and not-for-profit worlds will complain to me that they just don't understand what these young people want. I hear, "Why aren't they volunteering for committees or participating at a higher level in the organization?" Then I ask those clients to look around the room at the people to their left and their right. How many of them are under the age of fifty-five or sixty? When was the last time any of them personally extended the invitation to someone under forty or thirty to serve at the higher levels? Usually, they reply that they are waiting for those younger people to get more seasoning. But when I ask them how old they were when they took on their first significant leadership role on a charity board or professional committee, they remember with astonishment that they were about thirty-two years old.

Baby Boomers often get into the rut of thinking of themselves as the young rising energy of the new generation. While it was extremely true in its time, I hate to be the bearer of bad news, but Baby Boomers, you are over forty now. It's time to invite the new young voices to sit at the table with you and encourage them to express their views with the egalitarian weight that you fought so hard for in your thirties.

When you invite in Gen Xers and Millenials, however, be ready for them to bring in fresh ideas, tools, solutions, and an ASAP timeline to the problems you have been anguishing over for years. They will be ready to jump in and collaborate with energy and can-do enthusiasm. The quickest way to shut them down, turn them off, and ensure that they start looking for a new place to work, volunteer, or play is to respond with comfortable standby lines such as:

- We tried that before and it never worked.

- We've always done it this way.

- You haven't been here long enough to know this, but....

- It it's not broken, don't try to fix it.

- You're not old enough to remember this....

- Hey, kiddo, that's a really nice thought; I remember when I was your age…. (You start talking about yourself at length.)

MENTOR VS. MANAGER

Mentor core skills:

- Listening empathetically

- Questioning, using both open- and close-ended questions

- Giving candid, diplomatic feedback

- Providing both encouragement and challenges

Mentees first need to access:

- Their skill levels

- Interest areas

- Career goals

- Knowledge about the organization

- Personal development goals

Starters:

- I feel proud about my ability to…

- I know I will need to watch…

- I am looking forward to...

- I will be cautious about...

- What I want my coworkers to understand about me is...

- In my career, I want to...

MENTOR-UP ENVIRONMENT

It's easy to think that people younger than you don't have enough knowledge to understand the "complexities" the way you do, and that may be true to a point. However, leaders today are missing a key opportunity to capture both the creativity and loyalty of young people by not giving them an opportunity to "Mentor-Up."

The people side of the equation is where we need the Boomers and Traditionalists to mentor the Xers and Millennials. However, reverse mentorship comes into play when it comes to technology. We see a twenty-two-year old with tattoos and piercings mentoring a fifty-plus leader in a blue suit and starched color and tie.

Mentor-Up creates an informal or formal relationship where the younger person is recognized for his or her expertise in a particular area and encouraged to train older team members on that skill.

An opportunity for cross-generational bonding and understanding is to have Millennials design Mentor-Up workshops on a basic technology skill-set the team needs, and then hold a weekly mentoring session. Other formats for training can include short YouTube or internally hosted video trainings on high need skills like shortcuts or how to use a piece of software more effectively.

CREATING TRANSPARENCY FOR YOUR COMPANY

A healthy dose of skepticism in everything is the core thread running through the Xers' style of leadership. Xers can relate to Gregory House (on the Fox TV sitcom *House*) and his basic premise about management: "Assume everyone is lying." This philosophy keeps them safe and asking the hard questions. They grew up with a lot of empty promises from parents, advertisers, corporations, and national leaders. Because of this, Xers don't give respect based on tenure, title, or advertised brand promises. They are unfazed by authority that is bestowed upon someone. They trust experts who have proven their value in the field or on a project, or a peer who immediately shared the news that there was a good "guy or gal" or a great product at company XYZ that you can trust. Word travels fast through the Xers' e-mail ranks, both good and bad.

Transparency is a major hallmark of Gen Xers. They are asking to understand not only how they will be compensated by an organization, but how that organization makes its decisions and what are the rules and policies that organization lives and stands by. And when something goes wrong, they want to understand what went wrong, and why it went wrong. Even if that information and implementing solutions to prevent it from going wrong again go beyond their pay grade.

Things that keep Xers with your company include creating a safe environment for them to shine through mentorship, champions, and the sense of having a surrogate "family of origin." These criteria will keep your company afloat for the next generation as Traditionalists and Baby Boomers retire and Xers and Millenials take over the helm.

8

ENVIRONMENT

FROM SURVIVE TO THRIVE: WHAT WORKS FOR ~~WORK~~ "PLAY"

Expectations for what defines a work environment have undergone a radical transformation. A key question that today's top talent is asking when considering a new workplace is, "Will I thrive here?" It's no longer acceptable merely to survive your company, harassing boss, or jerk co-worker. Today's top talent wants your organization's environment to be a place where they will flourish and grow their skills.

Traditionalists didn't believe work was supposed to be the place you go to be happy, find fulfillment, and express your personality or life purpose. A Traditionalist says, "Work is called "WORK" for a reason. Work is a serious place you go to get a real day's work done."

In the 1930s and 1940s, work environment laughter on the job was a disciplinary offense. You could be sacked at the Henry Ford Motor Plant for smiling or whistling on the job. (Whistle while you work was a Disney-invented fantasy.)

Boomers entered the workforce desiring an egalitarian environment that allowed for a free flow of ideas and opinions, a Utopia. However, their formative experiences of competing for every opportunity with their Boomer peers quickly transformed each job, bid, and client opportunity into a game full of politics and intrigue to be won at all costs.

Xers entered the workplace with great trepidation, and today, they are viewing the demand that they move into higher levels of management with the same caution. For Xers, moving up the "ladder" means becoming the enforcer of environmental protocol and policies they don't believe in. Xers find navigating the political waters and intricate relationship mazes of the Baby Boomers exhausting and unfulfilling. They are creating their own environments that include: "No Jerk Policies" and "Results-Only Work Environments" (ROWE).

At the other end of the spectrum, the core of a Millennial's definition of work is: "Work is a personally fulfilling experience of creating a solution from wherever I am the most productive." For Millennials, work is a state of self-expression. It's not a place where you go to do something; it's what you do from wherever you are. They are looking for fun, friendly, and fast-paced environments that facilitate collaboration and rapid advancement.

LESSONS OF BEST PLACES TO WORK AND FASTEST GROWING COMPANIES

While leaders know the cost of talent-turnover is high, they often ignore the hard truth that it's frequently a problem they create. Today's talent expects to see fulfilled the "promised" company values and culture sold to them in the "romancing" interview stage of the courtship to stand up over time.

Xers and Millennials are clear that they spend the majority of their waking hours in their professional organization's environment. Whether or not they tell you so, top talent joins you on a trial basis all the while withholding judgment on how long they will stay. The ninety-day trial period is now a double-sided decision. If the answer to their question of thrive or survive is, "No, I will not thrive here," then they will begin looking, quietly, for a place where they will. Your investment of time, resources, and talent to attract the best and the brightest is wasted when you quickly lose them because they were sold on an environment the company couldn't or wouldn't provide.

FUN POSITIVELY IMPACTS THE BOTTOM LINE

Creating an environment that launches you into a "Fastest Growing Company" has a lot in common with being recognized as one of the "Best Places to Work."

Despite the tough economy, fast growing companies are not relying on the philosophy, "Our people are here because they have no other choice." Fastest Growing Companies' executives often cite as a core guiding principle, "People are our greatest asset." We accomplish great things because of our people.

"Best Places to Work" that are featured in business journals and magazines consistently report one three letter word that is central to the values of winning companies: "FUN." Yes, fun is profitable. Best Places to Work fun environments include the following common elements:

- Family friendly: Support active parenting practices

- Pet Friendly: Pet Policy allows bringing dogs to work

- Corporate Social Responsibility (CSR) is more than lip service

- Supportive of Volunteering: Financially and Philosophically

- Flexible: Workspaces (Virtual), Time-schedule (4/10 hour days, 3-day work weeks)

- Meritocracy: Rewards based on Results, not Tenure

- Technology Forward: Provide Budget of Professional Technology Upgrades

PAY FOR PERFORMANCE: ROWE

Xers and Millennials are increasingly comfortable with the "pay for performance" model. They are looking for environments where the performance expectations are clearly articulated and measurable. As technology continues to widen the gap in how we approach problems, and the time and resources needed to complete a task vary greatly (often depending on an individual's technical capacity), the demand by top performers is, "Don't measure me on face time or hours; measure me on deliverables and results."

My G.I. Generation mentor often recounts a work story of learning the hard way to play the measurement game. Early in his career, he was working at a state university's physical plant. His first day on the job, he was taken to a room piled with chairs to the ceiling that needed to be reupholstered. The team foreman asked him whether he could do the job. He had worked in a furniture factory on the east coast and was an expert at upholstery. Three days later, he found the foreman to report the job was done. The foreman was visibly upset. My G.I. generation friend didn't understand. He had done the job with speed and efficiency. The foreman said, "Don't you know that job was supposed to take you all summer? You were supposed to stretch it out. We pay based on hours, not on speed." This mindset can be a great frustration to those who just want to be measured on performance, not on time. Similarly, a Gen Xer friend of mine was hired in the early 1990s (one of his first jobs) by a company as a temp worker to retype a bunch of old typewritten documents onto a computer to create an ongoing database. He had a good work ethic and could type fast. He was also paid by the hour. He quickly realized that he could have made more money at the temp job if he had typed slower since he was getting paid the same per hour for 40 wpm as 60 wpm. The harder he worked, the sooner he was unemployed. Again, had he been paid for performance (perhaps each page typed) rather than by the hour, the situation would have been fairer. He learned that what he defined as good work ethic was costing him big time.

GEN XER AMY

Gen Xer Amy, a professional sales representative, had a great idea for a new application that would create an entire new revenue stream for her company, a billion dollar, search-engine solution that's revenue model was based on advertising. She floated the idea to her manager, who told her to write it up. She put together a report on the idea and submitted it. The organization reviewed it, implemented it, and created an entirely new million dollar revenue stream.

What did Amy, a high performer sales professional, get for creating something entirely outside her job description? Nothing, nada, zip, zilch, zero. Not only was this situation a missed opportunity for the giant company to highlight how it was a great company to work for because it valued, supported, and rewarded its team members for creative problem-solving and revenue-generating ideas, but worse, Amy's Boomer boss informed her that any idea she had while working for them was theirs—her innovation and intellectual capital were considered as the company's work product.

Gen Xer Amy learned her lesson. Now she keeps her ideas to herself and is looking for a new place to work that will value her as a partner, not a pawn.

Generationally Savvy Tip: Xers in particular want to be rewarded on performance-based models like ROWE (Results-Only Work Environment). They look for leaders who can create clarity around the needs, goals, and outcomes required to get the job done, and then fairly measure results based on it.

To meet this need for showing appreciation, showcase stories on your website, in your recruiting materials, and in social media outlets of how innovative solutions from team partners were implemented and individuals were rewarded for their contributions.

NO JERKS ALLOWED

With a "No Jerks Policy," the core practice at these companies is "Be a JERK and you are gone." Xers (and Millennials too) believe that life is too short to work with jerks. It takes courage to let them go, but Xers will respect and be loyal to leaders with the chutzpa to take courageous action.

Letting a toxic team member remain damages more than that person's own personal output. It erodes the rest of the team's belief in you as a leader and they will leave you over it.

I Believe In YOU—And I'll Provide You Cover

If you want to win the loyalty of a Gen Xer, you will need to demonstrate that you are a trustworthy individual. Xers know that companies are not people. Companies are made up of individual people, and they actively look for one "champion" or "mentor" who will provide cover for them in the workplace. They are incredibly loyal to that individual, not because of the person's title or function but due to his or her character. Company leaders would be wise to become aware of these informal alliances because they are where the real loyalty lies.

Xers put a lot of effort into keeping under the radar, and their mentors help with that. If the mentor or champion leaves the company and another alliance is not immediately created, the talented Xer is now in the high-risk category of leaving the company. Because Xers' alliances are to individuals and not to the organization, it's critical that these relationships are fostered and supported.

Xers know that the winds can change in the professional world at anytime, so their jobs are never "safe." There is always the possibility of something cataclysmic happening that could put them out on their own again. As a result, they always keep their resumes updated and are always looking for new bullet points that make them marketable.

Status and climbing the ladder the fastest or at all is not the same motivator to Xers as it was for Baby Boomers. They are discussing these opportunities with their spouses by asking questions such as, "Do we really need the money? Would the monetary increase balance out the quality of life costs like loss of personal time, time with children, and overall wellbeing?" The midlife natural progression to more time in the office and on the road that Boomers relished is just a potential garnish to Xers and one they may choose to eat their professional meal without. As one Boomer said about companies considering promoting Xers, "While you think you've nailed down your future, they are planning to open their own business when the politics get too much."

Loyalty to the company is a two-way street, and Xers know it is one often fraught with strings attached.

Generationally Savvy Solution: Answer for yourself, "How do you I employ the 80/20 rule?" Do you spend 80 percent of your time managing the problem child and only 20 percent managing the rest of the team and developing the top producers? Jerks create an energy vortex around them and consume excessive amounts of their colleagues and leaders' time and resources in managing or avoiding them. Do you take the courageous path to remove them from the team?

ANSWER THE TOUGH QUESTIONS

- What do we measure? Face-Time, Political Savvy, or Results?

- Do we truly support our managers?

- How do we measure effective leadership performance?

- Are we straight about our corporate culture to potential hires?

- Do we mentor our young leaders?

- Do we reward or penalize honesty?

- How is our environment and culture conducive to attracting and keeping Xers and Millennials?

- How much will it cost us to continue doing "business as usual"?

- How are we responsible for the loss of top talent?

TO MEET OR NOT TO MEET—THAT IS THE QUESTION

Among Gen Xers and Millenials, a major source of friction and @*&*%$ (complaining) is the number of meetings called by Baby Boomers to review, discuss, process, or just spend face-time with no clear agenda. For Xers, the very last thing they want to do is waste time in a nonessential meeting that does not have a clearly stated outcome or a timeline to accomplish that outcome. Even worse is holding a meeting that is just an exercise.

While they have suffered in silence, Xers often are voting with their feet. They are leaving the meetings or calling in and doing work on their computers while listening to "everyone weigh in and have a voice" as they make their way through the meeting. They will spend their time adding up the hourly rates of everyone in the meeting, calculating the time spent traveling to and from the meeting, and figuring out whether it's providing value equal to the cost.

One way for Xers and Millennials to try to survive the unproductive nature of meetings is to be able to keep working through their portable technology. Eye contact is a casualty, but productivity and spirit do not suffer quite as much. It comes down to what you measure and whether you value face time or output.

A Gen Xer client was serving on the board for a prestigious non-profit organization. She was the only Gen Xer in a room of fifteen Boomers and two Traditionalists. The Boomer President of the Board introduced a controversial political topic to the board for discussion with the directive to decide whether the board should openly support the initiative. For forty-five minutes of the one hour meeting, the board members hotly debated the issue with tempers rising. At the debate's end, with a positive vote to support the initiative, the president announced that the organization had a policy in place that prevented their participation, but he had wanted to give everyone a chance to voice their opinion. The Xer board member was enraged that forty-five minutes of time had been wasted for an egalitarian exercise the Boomer thought was fun.

YOU DIDN'T REMIND ME!

Boomer Nancy was in shock. Her Millennial rising star had failed to show up at a big client pitch with no warning or explanation. When she called Millennial Nicole into her office to get to the bottom of it, she heard something she never expected. Millennial Nicole said, "You forgot to remind me about the meeting."

Millennials are still coming to the meetings, but you may have to remind them about it. Their helicopter parents reminded them dozens of times about appointments, schedules, and practices in person and by text.

Generationally Savvy Solutions:

- What are the real takeaways from your meetings?

- How many meetings are essential, and how much is tradition or habit?

- Do you put the appropriate planning into the meeting to get the financial investment of hours back in equal or greater value?

- Is the face-to-face meeting integral to producing the outcome?

- Does everyone leave with a documented action item list that
he or she will be called to account for later?

- Do we share the reward of a good idea fairly?

MULTITASKING: RUDE OR EFFICIENT?

A frequent source of conflict and exasperation for many managers
and leaders with whom I consult is the way Millennials multitask at
work. Multitasking is often interpreted by Traditionalists and Boomers as not paying respectful attention to the person, meeting, or customer with whom they are working. This reaction comes as a surprise
to Millennials who never meant to be rude. Millennial feels strongly
that they need to—and are effective at—using multiple modes of
communication simultaneously.

The scientific merits of multitasking and time-management techniques are argued at length in other books and articles, so I won't do
that here. However, what is critical for people working with Millennials to understand is that no matter where you fall on the argument
of multitasking being effective, Millennials believe they can multitask and will proceed to do it whether you agree or not.

FILTERING FOR RELEVANCE

Currently, the estimation is that an individual sees 3,000-7,000
images or advertisements a day, emerging through video games, computers, digital music, digital images, and the Internet, along with lots
and lots of television. You don't hear Millennials complaining about
information overload because they are ignoring most of it. While
other adults are frustrated by the number of text messages, instant

messages, e-mails, and voicemails coming at them, Millennials are rapidly sorting through complex and sometimes massive amounts of information at proficiency levels many adults feel are impossible.

Millennials have grown up with multitasking as a natural reality; instant messaging while doing homework, texting while watching a video, listening to their iPod while reading, chatting with friends on Facebook while eating. They have trained themselves to work and "watch" programs on their digital devices, tuning in their attention only at the critical points in the storyline. They don't see it as a rude or distracting activity like it can be perceived by others. To a Millennial, having your earbuds in on the way to a meeting or while working on a project on the computer or walking down the hall is absolutely acceptable. It's what they've done all their lives. To their colleagues, it can look like they are in self-induced comas.

Generationally Savvy Solutions: Multitasking is a natural reality for Millennials. In a Survey U study, college students report multitasking 45 percent of the time. At best, you will get divided attention from Millennials as a default. To make sure your Millenials are paying attention when you want them to, follow these guidelines:

- Be explicit when earbuds are acceptable in your environment

- Clarify whether using mobile phones for texting is allowed during meetings

- Provide consistent role modeling and examples of the behavior you require. (Remember the ole' "Do as I say, not as I do" will not fly well with Millennials.

- Be rigorous about making meetings productive and well worth the time invested by each person to be off-line, off-the-grid, or unreachable. Those texts and IM's are not all personal.

BUSINESS DRESS PROTOCOL: BUSINESS FORMAL TO INFORMAL FLIP-FLOPS

No longer do employees have an implicit understanding of "professional protocol expectations." The examples Traditionalists and Boomers saw in action during their childhoods and early careers have disappeared. Many Millennials had nominal training at home or in college that required self-restraint, putting others first, or polite etiquette. In a 2011 Society for Human Resource Management study, the top concerns managers had about younger workers included inappropriate dress and poor work ethic.

Today, leaders need to recognize that training new talent to recognize and implement your professional protocols such as business dress is part of the job. While I was consulting for a national healthcare organization, an elegantly coifed female Boomer manager, with apparent frustration in her voice, said, "Okay, I'm going to address the elephant in the room. What about dress code? These young people think they can wear just any old thing and get away with it. Even when they are meeting with clients, they still look like they are in their pajamas." Clearly this was a huge point of pain and irritation for her as it is for many Boomers.

The business dress policy is something that can be a sore point for the older generations because it seems to be something that they each feel is obvious. Unfortunately, their perspective of what is obvious is not necessarily what the other generations think relevant.

For our Traditionalists who came of age with the military uniform being in popular vogue, they went to work dressing formally. For them, the appropriate dress code was a Brooks Brothers suit or a pin-striped suit with two or three buttons being the norm. Sometimes it was double-breasted, but it was always a suit with a tie, a jacket, slacks, and a shiny pair of shoes.

Baby Boomers thought it was a huge success when they changed the business dress code to include business casual, which included the options of blazer and slacks or a tie and suit for the most formal meetings.

Xers took it (up or down another level depending on your generational viewpoint) to more casual than business. They introduced the blazer and jeans and casual Fridays. The dot-com world advanced this agenda more quickly because the technology savvy Xers were highly sought after, and if what they demanded were blazers and jeans, then blazers and jeans it would be. Casual Fridays are something that many generations have come to enjoy.

Millennials have been allowed, and in fact, encouraged to use their dress as personal self-expression, and organizations that get frustrated by Millennials' lack of understanding are working on the assumption that Millennials have not been exposed to or educated to know anything else.

But in the movies, on TV, and in their own personal experiences in the workforce, or in their parents' expression of the workforce, they may have never been exposed to the business formal of the Traditionalists or even the business casual of the Baby Boomers. They may have only seen the casual of the Xers.

Millennials have taken the workplace from casual to comfy. Millennials come to work ready to express their personal style and viewpoints freely in their choice of wardrobe from flip-flops to pajama bottoms. Millennials feel they should be comfortable as they do the job. In their minds, as long as no one sees them dressed that way, what's the big deal?

KNOW YOUR AUDIENCE: DRESS FOR THE CLIENT

Boomers and Traditionalists know the adage, "We dressed for the job we want, not the job we have." If Xers and Millenials are seeking to move upward and garner respect from senior generations in the workplace, they need to take their dress code cues to heart. How you dress means a lot to your client, customer, or audience in any forum.

Being respected by a Boomer or a Traditionalist involves integrating their dress codes into your wardrobe choices. It may include ladies wearing plain nylons and closed toe shoes with a business suit. Gentlemen, when approaching a senior Boomer or Traditionalist, it will be wise to wear a suit, and tie, not a jacket, open-collared shirt, and slacks.

COSTUMING 101

Even if you see a peer attorney going to work in skinny jeans with spike heels and a jacket, don't assume that behavior is not affecting her future. While it may be the current style and her personal self-expression, if her clients are Boomers, Traditionalists, (and often Xers) she is losing credibility with them.

When your organization feels that it's extremely important to have a very formal or a very structured business dress code, it actually needs to take the time to train the Millennials about what the dress code means for you. One way of getting them this training is to use the metaphor of preparing for a role in a movie. For example, when I was coaching Millennial Tammy in her preparation for a college admissions interview and I asked what she planned to wear for the big event, Tammy responded, "I'm planning on my new Lucky jeans and the new Abercrombie & Fitch sweatshirt I bought last week." This was clearly her idea of showing her personal style.

Instead of arguing the merits of her choices, I asked her another question. I queried, "What kind of student do you think the university is going to be looking for in the interview?" Tammy immediately responded, "A student leader. I've got that covered in my application." I continued by putting my question into context. I said, "Say you are in a movie and you wanted the audience immediately to know your character's role. How would you costume your actress who is portraying a student leader?" Tammy's ideas flowed, "I would have her wear that long black pencil skirt and a crispy white blouse with my vest." She continued now speaking of herself, "I should also wear my hair in a ponytail to look more serious and my black-rimmed reading glasses make me look smarter!"

DRESS CODE PREFERENCES:

TRADITIONALISTS: Formal Brooks Brothers

BABY BOOMERS: Business Casual "Preferred"—no tie

GEN XERS: Casual Jeans—Casual Fridays, Jeans Day with blazer

MILLENIALS: Comfortable Living: flip-flops, personal expression, pajamas

Generationally Savvy Solution: Take time to establish context and allow for creative collaboration around the reasons for the protocol or policy. Too often, the rationale of "We've been doing it this way for one hundred years" is expected to be enough to commandeer compliance. While it may have sufficed in the past, it will not have the same effect today. Instead of pitting yourself against the Millennials and turning everything into a fight for self-expression or self-suppression, proactively examine your current policies, protocols, and practices for their practicality and relevance in how you do business today. Ask the tough questions:

- Is this protocol/policy still relevant?

- Are there situations where it no longer applies?

- Is the cost of enforcing it more than the payoff of having it?

CREATE YOUR SPACE FOR PLAY

Millennial Sarah

New professional Millennial Sarah was miserable on her first week of work. Instead of spring-boarding from her college graduation into her challenging new career, she was depressed and lonely. There was no one to hang with and talk to while at work. She had been so excited to get the job, but when she arrived in the office each morning, her new team members went directly into their offices and closed their doors to work.

By Friday, Millennial Sarah was desperate. She called her brother to commiserate and figure out what to do for lunch. She couldn't bear eating alone again. He suggested she go to the library down the street from her office that had a cool cafe and lots of people around to watch. Sarah arrived at the cafe at noon. As she sat down at a table, she noticed the chair across from her being pulled out. Sarah looked up and saw her brother sitting down to keep her company.

While Xers have a high tolerance for independent work in isolation, Millennials grew up working in groups, pairs, quads, and teams. Millennials thrive in friendly, warm environments that facilitate team members connecting and social engagement.

The gray, utilitarian cubicle work solution that evolved to address the flood of Boomers into the workforce no longer fits the required creative space needs. The instructions to think outside the box ring a little hollow when you are literally working in a box.

In the workplace, Millennials prefer to have areas where they can plop, crash, and create together in an informal space. The corner office with a closed door, nameplate, and corporate title is not the same motivator or symbol of status for Xers and Millennials that it was for Boomers and Traditionalists. Instead, it has become a form of torture for a Millennial to be disconnected from his or her peeps, peers, and friends.

PARADIGM SHIFTS IN THE WORK ENVIRONMENT

- Boomers and Traditionalists like to mark their space with pictures of family, education, and awards

- Xers appreciate the lack of physical hierarchy reinforcement through square footage

- Xers bring their family with them everywhere on their digital devices: iPhone, iPad, Droid

- Millennials don't see the need for separate space to hold paper documentation. With earbuds and iTunes or Pandora, anywhere can become a private place to work—a good thing because with four generations in the workplace, there is no chance of finding a music channel that appeals to everyone.

- Four walls may create privacy, but they don't allow for creative intimacy.

ON DEMAND LEARNING

For our Millennial, it's an on demand world. Learning may be our way of life, but we need to make it fun. On my time, in my way. Millennials became the "on demand" generation: "When I'm ready, I want to have the information available to me." They need knowledge broken down in chunks, not delivered to them in large massive quantities but in bite-size, adjustable, small snippets of information.

Millennials want an active and fully-engaged training model; they are not content to remain passive learners in their own development.

As Millennials enter the workplace, they have come out of an environment designed around catering to their needs, desires, and learning styles. Private and public high schools and colleges have competed to win their tuition by constantly upgrading their systems and revising their policies to address the new wrinkles raised by the digital natives' expectations.

Generationally Savvy Solutions: Create a curriculum of Stretch Assignments—to apply skills, employees need to learn to advance in the organization. Senior and high-potential mid-level leaders can provide coaching and mentoring on the projects. Emerging talent can be identified to participate in the Stretch Curriculum or self-identify and apply to participate.

The lecture stand-and-deliver method—where passive individuals simply listen and learn, and which Boomers and Traditionalists have come to expect and respect—will not be enough to engage and energize the full potential of the younger generations. Millennials have been learning in full-spectrum environments with hands-on, interactive, and practical examples including:

- web-based learning

- iPads to learn at their time and location of choice

- iPods

- smart phones

- digital devices

- face-to-face

- webinars

- online courses

- avatars

- distance learning

- podcasts

Millennials expect their new bosses and employers to have consistent standards for providing the latest and greatest digital technology available. Ready or not, here they come.

9

SUCCESS

Success is the culmination of the first four elements of Generational CODES. Our success is determined by taking the information we have learned about the generations and applying it to benefit the workplace, our relationships, and everyone involved. Success is the result of properly positioning our benefits, measurements, rewards, and reasons for doing what we do. There is no magical "Silver Bullet" that will make "Today's Kids" or "The Old Folks" suddenly see the world correctly (aka from your perspective). The magic happens when we learn how to see the world from their perspectives, appreciating or at least understanding those perspectives, and translating our words and thoughts into their own, understanding where they are coming from so we can get us and them where we want our business and our relationships to go.

Now that we have the knowledge we need to understand different generations and their CODES, we're ready to apply it to our efforts for success.

QUESTIONS ABOUT WHAT DEFINES SUCCESS

Success for leaders of tomorrow comes from understanding each generation's answers and the reasons for those answers (even if we don't agree with them) to the questions:

- What does my measurement for professional and personal success include?

- What things am I willing and not willing to give up to achieve that success?

- What internal and/or external factors influence my definition of success?

- What do I want from my job/career?

- What do I expect my boss/leader/coach/mentor to provide?

- What inspires my loyalty in the workplace?

COMMON POINTS OF GENERATIONAL FRICTION THAT AFFECT SUCCESS

You may have come across one (or more) of these common Friction Points:

Work Culture

- What's expected: formality/informality?

- What's acceptable? How much flexibility?

- How does the professional dress code look?

Work Ethics

- What does a "real" day of work include?

- How much willingness is there to expend extra/discretionary effort to get the job done?

Organizational Hierarchy

- Challenging or questioning someone from an "older" generation

Technology Issues

- Ever-increasing volume and speed of information and gadgets/programs

Managing Change

- Change-management skills and comfort levels with change vary by generation

Respect

- Beliefs about other generations' lack of respect for my values and beliefs

THE AREAS OF IMPACT ON SUCCESS

An organization that creates a positive, generationally-inclusive culture can experience enhanced recruitment success, improved talent retention, and increased profitability. By supporting strong communication and understanding between all the generations, businesses see the impact in a number of areas:

- Increased respect for the contribution and value of talent of all ages.

- Decreased "brain drain"—key competitive knowledge is shared more efficiently.

- Improved results in recruitment as messages are uniquely tailored to attract people from each generation.

- Enhanced succession planning as younger managers see a longer-term future possible.

- Higher employee satisfaction as individuals come to believe that career development opportunities are accessible and equal for people of all ages.

- Decreased training costs as retention rates improve and inter-generational mentorship programs succeed.

- Expanded customer satisfaction and loyalty as effectiveness in appealing to the needs of each generation improves.

- Improved customer service experiences as all ages learn what the expectations and needs of each generation include.

The successful leader and coach of the future must be savvy when it comes to recognizing the Generational CODES and cues of their clients, customers, or partners. And once those CODES are identified, the leader must subtly blend his or her own generational style with the preferences of those they are seeking to serve (and have serve them as employees).

Visually we often have the advantage of getting a pretty accurate guess of an individual's generational origin. Knowing the other cues can be helpful such as:

- A Traditionalist who seems to be obsessively focused on dress code infractions as a personal slight. An eighty-plus customer who is offended by the young person shouting out a greeting as she enters the boutique clothing store.

- A Boomer sharing his career success and professional political prowess with endless enthusiasm for hearing his own stories. A sixty-plus executive referring collectively to a group of individuals ranging from their thirties to sixties as "people our age."

- A Gen Xer focusing all her resources and time on her Nexter kids. A forty-plus executive approaching a business development conversation with an awkward or abrupt demeanor that seems rude to the mid-fifties potential client.

- A Millennial who expects to have time off to go on a family vacation within the first three months of his employment. A twenty-plus client who is offended by receiving a marketing package with lots of non-recyclable promotional materials.

Your capacity to embrace and integrate others' Generational CODES to customize your sales message, customer service, leadership, and the opportunities you have to give can make all the difference.

Today, thriving in the workplace is always a balancing act. Everyone is grappling with work/life balance. Here is how the various generations are performing that balancing act to survive and thrive:

- Traditionalists' increased lifespan is putting extreme demands on their limited financial resources, requiring them to explore how to stay relevant as technology to which they have never been exposed is rapidly taking over as the solution.

- Boomers are the "sandwich generation" with aging parents in need of increasing medical care and boomerang Millennial children returning to the nest after college. Boomers who thought they would be relaxing and exploring new horizons are staying in the workplace on average nine years longer than planned.

- Xers want to spend premium time with their young Nexter children, but they are struggling with increasing career demands as they reluctantly deal with mid-life management. Frustration mounts as the Boomers' professional pause from work creates a bottleneck in leadership movement and technological adaptation.

- Millennials are confused that the consistent flow of positive messages fed to them by their parents, teachers, and coaches has suddenly slowed to a trickle or been turned off entirely. As they leave the safe haven of school and plunge into the icy cold labor pool, they are seeking mentorship and training to develop their future plans.

If you've read this far in the book, you should now have all the tools you need to understand and work with the different generations in today's workplace. You may still not have all the answers, but you have the tools to help you find those answers. For easy reminders, at the back of this book I've included a quick-and-easy reference guide summing up the book's main points about the Generational CODES.

I wish you a successful, inspired, fun and meaningful experience in your relationships with members of all generations.

And when something doesn't work out, remember:

It's not personal—it's generational.

But I trust by now, you already know that!

May you live to see many more generations!

The Keys to Generational CODES:
A QUICK AND EASY REFERENCE GUIDE

KEY TOOLS

1. RESPECT: Every generation deserves RESPECT for how it sees the world.

2. Remember the Mantra: It's not personal. It's Generational.

3. Basic Generational Principle #1: No Generation is Right or Wrong.

4. Basic Generational Principle #2: Understand that each generation assumes (until educated in Generational CODES) that it is right and other generations are wrong, simply because it does not understand the other generations.

BIG PICTURE: MULTI-GENERATIONAL MIX PERSPECTIVE FOR SUCCESSFUL MANAGERS

- Flexible: Lots of options for people to choose from

- Open: Lots of communication about differing perspectives

- Responsive: Meets individuals' needs and preferences

- Positive: Expects the best from everyone

- Diverse: Consciously seeks a variety of perspectives

- Developmental: Helps people to advance in their chosen careers/investing goals

- Retention-Oriented: Focuses daily on keeping good people/clients

- Hire Slow—Fire Fast: Is slow to hire talent and quick to fire jerks and energy vampires

TOP TIPS FOR GENERATIONAL SAVVY LEADERS

1. Feedback is Key. Like it or not, Millennials want frequent positive feedback.

2. Social Media is mission critical to communications, not a frivolous fad.

3. Multitasking is a way of living and working for Millennials and (Xers too).

4. Dress codes need to have a purpose, not be a legacy habit.

5. People are planning to change their jobs. Deal with it, and Plan for it.

6. Careers are about knowledge skill sets, not titles.

7. Today work is defined by what solution you create, not where you create it.

8. What motivated you is only that. Don't expect it to be what motivates other generations.

9. Yes, Millennials are confident and have high expectations of life and their careers.

10. You can resist other generations all you want, but it's not a productive use of your energy.

GENERATIONAL WORKPLACE TICKS, TICK-OFFS, AND SO...WHAT TO DO'S

SALES

	Tick	Tick Off	So...What To Do
TRADITIONALIST	Be Respectful Observe Protocol Organized Thinking Personal Touch In-Person Meetings Print Materials	Pressure Slick Off The Cuff Cavalier Attitude E-mail Only	Make first contact formal—a peer or colleague they already know. Send questions ahead of time to allow them to prepare. Serve coffee, make formal introductions. Gold-embossed materials and thick folders. Demonstrate your organization with structured agenda. Present purpose of the meeting and process that you propose to use. As a courtesy, call the client to inform him or her when you send e-mails.
BOOMER	Relationship focus Processes Dialogue Face-to-Face Schmoozing Formal Presentation Consensus	Technology Passing the Buck Impatience Poor Follow-up Slow Service	Understand that the whole process is interpersonal; it's all about the relationship building. Ask questions to help Boomer get clarity about issues. Send questions ahead of time and bring backup copies. Schedule face-to-face meetings. Be patient; it may take awhile to get on their calendar. Be ready to present "formally" to team of 3-10. Decisions generally take weeks if not months. Boomers expect support from the person who sold them the business.

	Tick	Tick Off	So...What To Do
GEN XER	Business First Brevity Value Up Front Short responses 20-Minute Meetings Answer "WIIFM?" 24-hour turnaround	Being Personal Hard Pitch Small Talk Jargon Wasting Time "How's it going?"	Talk about business opportunities up front. Respond and send e-mails early in the morning. Be ready for them to give you 5-15 minutes to pitch on the spot. Don't just come in and ask soft, personal non-business questions; it drives Xers nutty. Show you did your research. They will have done theirs on you. Demonstrate immediate value, bottom-line payoffs for them. Present in their office. Show respect by efficiently using their time. Be prepared to present to one person. Don't be overly familiar before you provide value. Focus meeting to answer their question, "What's in it for me?" Be efficient; no bogus "how's it going" follow-up calls.
MILLENIAL	Social Media Facebook YouTube Text Messaging Collaborative Tone Snap-Shot Solutions Peers Parents as BFFs	Long Voicemails Long E-mails Waste of Paper Rigid Structure	Connect electronically: Facebook is home base. Cell phones are for Caller ID; texting is better. They only have e-mail (as a necessary evil) for work purposes. Take a collaborative/learning approach. Send questions ahead of time to let them do their research. Present information in visual format, not prose. Deliver information and supporting documentation electronically. Be open to including their cohorts or parents in the process. Be prepared; they will Google/Bing you to do due diligence.

LEADERSHIP

	Tick	Tick Off	So…What To Do
TRADITIONALIST	Battle Plan Contingency Plan Chain of Command Marching Orders	Disrespect Attitude Being Touchy-Feely Indecisiveness Greed Breaking rules for personal gain Going around the boss	Approach: Directive, Logical, Authoritative Plan: Clear, Precise, Long-Term Goal Style: Authoritative, Due Respect, Distant
BOOMER	Group Roll-Out Mission Statement Driven Attitude Data Rich Rewards/Incentives	Bureaucratic "my-way-or-the-highway" attitude People who question "their rules" People taking away their perks and packages Questioning their ethics	Approach: Consensual, Democratic, Process-Driven Plan: Work with the "designated" group to define vision/mission Style: Friendly "equals" open to input from appropriate leadership peers
GEN XER	I trust you to get the job done on time, as promised. Here's the bottom-line. Your resources are A, B, & C. Your deliverables are X & Y. The deadline is Z. Any questions?	Micromanagement People not walking their talk	Approach: Competence, Results-Oriented Plan: Project, Deadline, & Give People the Freedom to get it done Style: Informal, Genuine, Bottom-Line
MILLENIAL	Collaboration and excitement Working in groups, pods, crews where everyone gets a chance to play Acknowledgment for trying	Cynicism "Kiddo" name-calling or tone Technophobia	Approach: Collaborative, Experiential, Digital Plan: Educational, Technically Savvy, "Gamer" Dive-In Style: Achievement-Oriented, Positive, Fast

SERVICE

	Tick	Tick Off	So...What To Do
TRADITIONALIST	Formal tone, polite language, both verbally and physically	Profanity Rudeness Indifference to your job performance Casual dress code Poor grammar Sloppy work	Use formal address: Sir, Miss Formally introduce yourself by title Invite them to call you by your first name. Identify your "rank" or "tenure" with the organization. Offer to have supervisor follow up after issue. Use positive language: "I'd be delighted to show you personally."
BOOMER	Interactive Interpersonal Values Recognition Listening to Them Personable Focused on THEM Authenticity	Brusqueness Unfriendliness Shows of power One up-manship	Address by first name or professional title if applicable. Ask about Millennial children's achievements. Use direct eye contact. Write down their ideas to show respect. Invite them to suggest a solution to an issue, "What do you think would be the best solution?" Offer personally to address the issue: "I'll personally make sure this is resolved."
GEN XER	Efficient Child-Friendly Blunt Immediate Action Instant Response Socially Brief Focused Straightforward Product-Focused Brief Authentic	Chatty Empty Words Overselling Service Incompetence Over-Promise Under-Deliver Perky—Fakery Buzzwords Lingo	Offer your services but give them room to explore. Don't hover or pressure them with details or information they did not request. Give them clear, concise facts that are benefits focused. Learn their children's name, interests, and hobbies. Relate to the parent through what advances their children. Admit what's true. Don't fake your expertise or the services or benefits. Immediately follow-up in a 24-hour timeframe.

	Tick	Tick Off	So...What To Do
Millenial	Collaborative Cheerful Participative Open/Sharing Positive Attitude Upbeat Energy Educational Approach	Slow Speed Single-Tasking Stiffness Formality Snide Tone Hovering	Give them space to look around and make their decision. Include their friends and parents in the process. Invite them to offer their suggestions. "Let's find the answer together." Appreciate their contribution to finding the solution. "When we work together like this with you, it improves the experience for everyone. Thank you."

PARADIGM SHIFTS ACROSS THE GENERATIONS

Company Man	→	Free Agent
Nationalist	→	Global Citizen
White Glove Service	→	Latex Gloves Transaction
Work is where you go	→	Work is what you do from wherever
Day One: Sink or Swim	→	Concierge Onboarding
Loyalty to the Company	→	Loyalty to Self
Protocols/Etiquette	→	Personal Self-expression
Chain of Command	→	No command
Authoritarian Parenting	→	Helicopter Parenting
Manage	→	Inspire
Bawling Out/Dressing-Down	→	Teachable Moments
Vetted Experts	→	User-Generated Content
Pinstripes Suits	→	Working in Your Pajamas
Going visiting (via a car)	→	Virtual visiting via digital highway

Alsop, Ron. *The Trophy Kids Grow Up: How the Millenial Generation is Shaking Up the Workplace*. San Francisco, CA: Jossey-Bass, 2008.

Beck, John C. and Mitchell Wade. *Got Game: How the Gamer Generation is Reshaping Business Forever*. Boston, MA: Harvard Business Press, 2004.

Erickson, Tamara. *Plugged In: The Generation Y Guide to Thriving at Work*. Boston, MA: Harvard Business School, 2008.

Johnson, Meagan and Larry Johnson. *Generations, Inc.: From Boomers to Linksters—Managing the Friction Between Generations at Work*. New York: American Management Association, 2010.

Lancaster, Lynne C. and David Stillman. *The M-Factor: How the Millenial Generation is Rocking the Workplace*. New York: HarperCollins, 2010.

Lancaster, Lynne C. and David Stillman. *When Generations Collide: Who They Are. Why They Clash. How to Solve the Generational Puzzle at Work*. New York: HarperCollins, 2002.

Marston, Cam. *Motivating the "What's In It for Me?" Workforce: Manage Across the Generational Divide and Increase Profits*. Hoboken, NJ: John Wiley & Sons, 2007.

Martin, Carolyn A. and Bruce Tulgan. *Managing Generation Y: Global Citizens Born in the Late Seventies and Early Eighties.* Amherst, MA: HRD Press, 2001.

Ryan, Rebecca. *Live First, Work Second.* Madison, WI: Next Generation Consulting, 2007.

Salkowitz, Rob. *Generation Blend: Managing Across the Technology Age Gap.* Hoboken, NJ: John Wiley & Sons, 2008.

Strauss, William and Neil Howe. *The Fourth Turning: What the Cycles of History Tell Us About America's Next Rendezvous with Destiny.* New York: Broadway Books, 1997.

Sujansky, Joanne and Jan Ferri-Reed. *Keeping the Millennials: Why Companies Are Losing Billions in Turnover to This Generation—and What to Do About It.* Hoboken, NJ: John Wiley & Sons, 2009.

Trunk, Penelope. *Brazen Careerist: The New Rules for Success.* New York: Warner Business Books, 2007.

Twenge, Jean M. *Generation Me: Why Today's Young Americans Are More Confident, Assertive, Entitled—and More Miserable Than Ever Before.* New York: Free Press, 2006.

Zemke, Ron, Claire Raines, and Bob Filipczak. *Generations at Work: Managing the Clash of Veterans, Boomers, Xers, and Nexters in Your Workplace.* New York: AMACON, 2000.

SOURCES

CHAPTER 1

1. http://assets.aarp.org/www.aarp.org_/cs/misc/leading_a_multi-generational_workforce.pdf Accessed September 8, 2011.

CHAPTER 3

1. These ages are based upon Piaget's Cognitive Development Theory.

2. DISC is an acronym for Dominance, Influence, Steadiness, and Compliance. These four dimensions can be grouped in a grid with "D" and "I" sharing the top row and representing extroverted aspects of the personality, and "C" and "S" below representing introverted aspects. "D" and "C" then share the left column and represent task-focused aspects, and "I" and "S" share the right column and represent social aspects. In this matrix, the vertical dimension represents a factor of "Assertive" or "Passive," while the horizontal dimension represents "Open" vs. "Guarded" (Wikipedia: http://en.wikipedia.org/wiki/DISC_assessment Accessed September 8, 2011).

CHAPTER 4

1. In Wolfe's 1977 book *Mauve Gloves & Madmen, Clutter & Vine*, which included Wolfe's famous essay, "*The Me Decade and the Third Great Awakening*."

CHAPTER 5

1. pewresearch.org/millennials/ Accessed September 8, 2011

CHAPTER 6

1. For the full thirty-two page survey report, visit: http://www. aplin.com/marketing/survey/Jun2008/GenXY-report.pdf Accessed August 28, 2011.

2. http://www.deloitte.com/view/en_US/us/Insights/Browse-by-Content-Type/deloitte-review/35912ee3fad33210VgnVCM100000 ba42f00aRCRD.htm Accessed August 30, 2011.

CHAPTER 7

1. http://www.showbizspy.com/article/221072/johnny-depp-didnt-like-kissing-angelina-jolie-for-movie.html Accessed August 28, 2011

RESULTANCE, INC.
CONSULTING SERVICES

Resultance, Inc. Consulting Services helps organizations improve productivity, profitability, and customer satisfaction and employee morale through integrated management coaching and custom training solutions.

Anna Liotta, CEO of Resultance Inc., has provided training and consultation on generational issues to hundreds of leaders and major professional associations in small businesses and multi-national corporations across the U.S. Anna's books, articles, trainings, and blog explain how Generational CODES affect every aspect of business, including recruiting and retention, management and motivation, and sales and marketing. Anna is passionately committed to helping organizations achieve higher productivity, improved morale, and better retention rates. She offers her clients practical solutions and lessons on improving communication so they may solve the generational issues that confront their specific industries. Anna has provided generational insight and advice to leadership at the nation's most prominent corporations, including Merrill Lynch, Microsoft, Whitepages.com, John L. Scott, Seattle Cancer Care Alliance, Wells Fargo, Group Health Cooperative, and Washington Association of Society Executives, Entrepreneurs Organization (EO), pwc (Price Waterhouse Coopers), and Parsons.

KEYNOTES

Anna Liotta is a highly popular speaker for corporate meetings, government conferences, and association meetings. She partners with clients and event planners to customize her keynote to address specific challenges facing each audience, whether they revolve around leadership/management issues, building stronger teams, or reaching four generations of customers.

Resultance, Inc. keynotes teach audiences how to:

Understand the four generations they partner with daily—Traditionalists, Baby Boomers, Generation Xers, and Millennials.

Recognize Generational Moments™ that reveal understanding of different generations' perspectives and how they may cause breakdowns and upsets.

Develop specific approaches for successfully recruiting, retaining, motivating, and managing a multi-generational workforce.

Design and implement succession planning and effective knowledge transfer for critical employees at every level in the organization.

Anna has also offered presentations and consultations for Parsons, Prudential, Port of Seattle, ING, RMS McGladrey, and the U.S.

Society of Military Engineers as well as major professional associations such as the American Bankers Association and the Executive Women International, Washington Bankers Association. She is an ongoing instructor at University of Washington Technical Management MBA.

RESULTANCE, INC.
GENERATIONALLY SAVVY
TRAINING INSTITUTE

Resultance, Inc. training programs will guide you to the premiere knowledge and resources.

Using best practices from her work across industries, Anna shares how today's most competitive companies are competing for, winning, and retaining their top people. Generationally Savvy workshops and trainings can be customized to be ½ day to full-day programs covering:

- Leadership Skills
- Sales Training

- Customer Service
- Marketing

- Communication
- Social Media

The Generationally Savvy Training Institute offers 2½ day customized intensive Train the Trainer in-house learning experiences on-site at your organization.

An annual The Resultance, Inc.® Train the Trainer Certification course delivered in Seattle gives you the content base, training techniques, classroom practice, and materials to structure and present generations educational sessions successfully in flexible formats.

ABOUT THE AUTHOR

Anna Liotta, creator of Generationally Savvy Communication Solutions™, is an award-winning speaker, consultant, and author who engages and energizes national audiences with her practical strategies for attracting, growing, and retaining top talent and loyal clients from every generation. Her unique interdisciplinary approach integrates the crucial elements of communications, sociology, business psychology, and demography. Her expertise and approach have helped such companies as Pike Place Fish, Microsoft, Seahawks, Intel, Wells Fargo, Office Max, United Way, Merrill Lynch, and the Federal Reserve Bank of San Francisco. Anna holds a Master's degree in Interpersonal Communication and has over fifteen years of experience in the field of intergenerational communication and leadership as a consultant, coach, speaker, and author. As an author, professor, and blogger, she imparts a clear understanding of how generational demographics are changing the landscape of business.

Honored by the Puget Sound Business Journal as one of the "Top 40 Business Leaders Under 40," Anna is an adjunct faculty member in the University of Washington's Executive MBA program, and she also serves as the chair of the institutional advancement committee on the board of trustees at Antioch University.

Anna's most impressive generational credential, however, is that she grew up in a household of six generations, making her daily life an "insider's view" into the realities of generational communication. In addition, she is one of nineteen children!

What that means, of course, is that for Anna, every family Thanksgiving, graduation, or wedding is a doctoral level course in generational communication. Anna is a native resident of Washington State and lives with her Labradoodle puppy, Golfing, in the Belltown neighborhood of Seattle with the Space Needle just outside her window.

For more information about Anna Liotta, visit her at:

www.UnlockingGenerationalCodes.com

www.Resultance.com

www.FullyFollow.Me/AnnaLiotta

ACKNOWLEDGMENTS

Anything we achieve is possible because of the support, and encouragement of our family and friends both professionally and personally. I am deeply grateful to the many people listed here who believe in me and my dreams. It is because of you this book has become a reality. Thank you.

Aaron Anderson

Al Liotta

Alex Bogaard

Annalee Luhman

Annette Fischer

Antioch Board of Trusteess

Auntie Mary Gritti

Beth Condon

Bill Boyd

Bill Center

Bill Stainton

Bob Jaxheimer

Bob Rosner

Bob Senoff

Carrie Heinrich

Brett Alston

Brian Hawksford

Brian Roundtree

Brian Walter

Buckley Buddies - Pete, Anne Marie, Jordan

Candy Lee

Cathy Karten

Charles Liotta

Chuck Heinrich

Cindy Runger Balas

Corriene Liotta

Daisaku Ikeda

Dan Diamond

Dan Zadra

Dana Manciagli

Dawn Matisse

Deanna Turner

Debbie Wege

Dennis Aherns

Dennis Goldstein

Diane Callahan

DJ Norman

Doris Quan

Dwyla Donahue

Eddie Pate

Emily West

Erick Slabaugh

Erika Schmidt

Evelyn Clark

Flora McGill

Frank Sunseri

Guy Byrd

Heidi Wills

Irene Coppa

Jan Dwyer Bang

Jay Gusick

Jeannie Powers

Jerry & Lois Levin

Jim Cleghorn

Jim Wheeler

Joanne Eng

Joe Thompson

John Callahan

John Thompson

Joseph Marra

Karen Orlando

Kelly Holm

Ken Colling

Ken Grant

Kobi Yamada

Kristen Juan-Snyder

Laura Stack

Lenora Edwards

Lisa Gritti

Lisa Pollman

Liz Powell

Luis Aguilar Lemarroy

Lynn Edwards

Lynne Walker

Maria Shindler

Maria Tringali

Mark Byrd

Mark Sanborn

Mathis Dunn

Matt Jones

Mauri Moore

Mike Byrd

NSA Buddies

NW Nexters

Othella Jones

Pat Harding

Patrick Snow

Patt Schwab

Patty Shadden

Paul Campbell

Randy Kim

Scott Friedman

Shelley Roberts

Sherry Lilienthal

Simon T. Bailey

Soka Gakkai International

Steve Crandall

Teresa Gritti

Teresa Hollis

The Antionettes

Kevin Knutson

Tom Hurdelbrink

Tyler Tichelaar

Vanna Novak

Wendy Alston

William Lampe

Yvonne Adams

Zoye Marinopoulou

IT'S NOT PERSONAL-
IT'S GENERATIONAL

RESPECT

IT'S THE VERY SIMPLE PRINCIPLE THAT IS AT THE HEART OF WHO WE ARE

AS HUMAN BEINGS.

WHILE EACH GENERATION IS UNIQUE IN ITS VIEWS, THEY ALL HAVE TWO

FUNDAMENTAL THINKS IN COMMON:

1. THEY ALL BELIEVE THEIR WAY OF SEEING THE WORLD IS RIGHT.

2. THEY ALL WANT RESPECT FOR HOW THEY SEE THE WORLD.

GENERATIONAL COMMON GROUND

SERIOUSLY?

ORDER FORM
GENERATIONALLY SAVVY PRODUCTS

INDIVIDUAL UNIT PRICING

Book	
_____	Single book ($24.95)
_____	Wholesale quotes available upon request
Generationally Savvy Cliff Notes Set of 4 Generations ($19.95)	
_____	Selling to the Generations
_____	Leading the Generations
_____	Customer Service for the Generations
Generational Office Art Individual Print ($4.95)	
_____	SERIOUSLY?
_____	It's Not Personal ~ It's Generational

CUSTOMER INFORMATION / METHOD OF PAYMENT

Customer Name:		
Company:	Non-Profit: yes	no
Address:		
City:	State:	Zip Code:
Phone:	Fax:	

NOTE: Products are also available for purchase online at www.resultance.com
or
www.UnlockingGenerationalCODES.com

_____	My check for $_____ is enclosed. Check #_____. (Make check payable to Resultance, Inc.)
_____	Please charge _____ registration(s) to the following credit card:
c Visa	c MasterCard	c Govt.
Card Number:	
Exp. Date: _____/ _____	3-Digit Security Code: _____
Card Holders Name:	
Billing Address:	
Signature:	

(206) 283-2905 ph • (206) 299-3235 fax • www.resultance.com
2515 Fourth Ave • Seattle, WA 98121

Please Note: Wholesale orders of Books, Generationally Savvy Cliff Notes and Generational Office Art are available upon request. Washington State taxes will be applied to all product sales.